AMERICAN POLITICAL SCIENCE

A profile of a discipline

The Atherton Press
Political Science Series

ATHERTON PRESS
70 Fifth Avenue
New York, New York 10011

AMERICAN
POLITICAL
SCIENCE
A profile of a
discipline

Albert Somit &
Joseph Tanenhaus

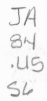

AMERICAN POLITICAL SCIENCE
Albert Somit & Joseph Tanenhaus

Atherton Press, 70 Fifth Avenue, New York, New York 10011

Library of Congress Catalog Card Number 64–25642
Printed in the United States of America 02856

Preface

The findings of this study were almost certain, given the questions posed, to vex a substantial number of our fellow political scientists. Knowing this, the reader may well wonder why we permitted ourselves to become involved in such an undertaking. The answer is very simple: like many other authors who find themselves in troubled waters, we originally charted a quite different course.

Our initial objectives called only for an analysis of the 1948, 1953, and 1961 directories of the American Political Science Association to ascertain possible trends within the profession. This line of inquiry soon led to a rueful conclusion—the three editions differed so fundamentally at critical points that meaningful comparisons were largely precluded.

At this point events took an unexpected turn. We received an invitation from Arnold Rogow, who had heard of our directory analysis from Harvey Mansfield, to read a paper on "Trends in American Political Science" at the forthcoming 1963 Association meeting. We were then faced with three options: to decline the invitation and drop our study altogether; to accept the invitation and present a paper based upon what little could be usefully gleaned from the directories; or to accept the invitation and then structure an investigation which would enable us to deal with what we thought were the truly important trends and issues confronting the discipline. Professional curiosity triumphed over discretion—and so this study came to be. Some preliminary findings went into the paper, which was duly read and subsequently published in *The American Political Science Review*. The great bulk of the data developed were later subjected to more intensive analysis and are reported here for the first time.

Large-scale questionnaire surveys of the type upon which we relied incur a vast indebtedness of gratitude. We would like to express our appreciation to the many persons who helped to facilitate our work. These include Paul Hamelberg, the director of New York University's Data Processing and Programming Center; three some-time associates in the University's Office of Institutional Research, Vina Barvicks, Paul Boerner, and Robert L. Lilienfeld; two extremely patient secretaries, Jaynie Goldstein and Dolores Prego; and two graduate assistants who contributed thought as well as labor, Roosevelt Ferguson and Khairy Abdel-Kawi. Our debt to H. L. Walowitz of the New York University Computing Center for permitting us to exploit his extraordinary knowledge of computers would be hard to overstate.

We owe much to the several dozen political scientists who commented with critical perception on our pretest questionnaire and no less to the several hundred members of the Association who responded to our inquiry. A number of persons aided us substantially by filling gaps in the available literature. In this regard we want specifically to thank Franklin L. Burdette, George P. Bush, and Wayne E. Tolliver of the Office of Education, Department of Health, Education, and Welfare.

At later stages we profited greatly, if not as much as we should have, from the comments and suggestions of Charles S. Hyneman, Harold D. Lasswell, and John C. Wahlke, who read our manuscript in penultimate draft. Allen Jossey-Bass and Maron Loeb of Atherton Press contributed lavishly of their skills and would have accomplished even more had it not been for the fanatical attachment which authors develop for their stylistic gaucheries.

Grants from the New York University Graduate School of Arts and Science Research Fund and the Ford Public Affairs Program provided the wherewithal for research assistants and for printing, mailing, clerical help, and computer costs. The study could not have been completed without this prompt and generous support.

From the foregoing it should be clear that our effort was in no way an official or an unofficial undertaking of the American Political Science Association. The Association did not sponsor or support the investigation and should be absolved of all responsibility for the contents of this volume.

Albert Somit

Joseph Tanenhaus

Contents

Tables and Charts

Chart

AMERICAN
POLITICAL
SCIENCE
A profile of a discipline

-1-
Introduction

This book is a case study of a single learned discipline—political science. As such, the volume will, no doubt, primarily interest members of that discipline. In this chapter however, we seek a broader frame of reference for two reasons. For one thing, most learned disciplines have a good deal in common. The other reason is that the disciplines are influential forces in the American system of higher education. Individually and collectively, they merit far more attention than they have received.

The analysis of anything as complex as a learned discipline must take into account a number of variables; therefore, most of the topics treated in this volume are related. Nevertheless, many readers may be interested in only selected aspects of this study. Hence, the chapter order was determined, in those instances in which alternatives were present, by a desire to accommodate those who do not plan to read consecutively. This order, however, is not always the most useful one for the task we have set ourselves in this introduction—placing the problems with which we deal in a wider perspective. We think this can be more meaningfully done by considering some of the main characteristics of a learned discipline and relating our study to them.

CHARACTERISTICS OF A LEARNED DISCIPLINE

A State of Mind

One characteristic of a learned discipline is a common state of mind. That is, the members of a discipline must think of themselves as belonging to a distinct and functioning profession. Such a state of mind can exist only if certain attitudes are widely shared. There must, for example, be substantial agreement on the areas of inquiry. The outer boundaries of any discipline are always difficult to identify with precision, but the subject matter of the core and the kinds of questions that may properly be asked about it are matters on which there must be general consensus. Among the more serious sources of potential discord in any discipline are the specialized fields of inquiry it spawns. Members of a discipline frequently find that their interests as specialists and their interests as members of the larger discipline are not identical. When these differences are severe, talk of secession becomes strident.

The state of mind essential for the existence of a discipline also requires substantial agreement on the methods appropriate for exploring its subject matter. If the members are not pretty much committed to a single best mode of inquiry, they must be willing to admit that the discipline is housed in a mansion roomy enough to accommodate a variety of methodologies. Discord over methods, like discord over scope, can pose a serious threat to a discipline.

But even consensus on scope and methods is not enough. If a discipline is to thrive, most of its members must be convinced that the work they are doing is truly meaningful. They must, for example, believe that the questions they ask are eminently worth asking and that the methods used in seeking answers to these worthy questions are reasonably suitable and productive. They must also believe that extending—or even merely transmitting—the discipline's knowledge and expertise is worth the mettle of mature and reflective individuals. And, if they were free to start all over and choose a career again, most members would need to feel that they would once more opt for their discipline.

As might be expected in a book primarily concerned with the values and perceptions of a discipline's membership, consensus and conflict over its fields, its scope, its methods, and the satisfaction derived from identification with it are major and recurring themes. They are discussed at various places in the chapters that follow, but especially in Chapters 2, 3, 6, and 12.

Formal Organization

A second characteristic of a learned discipline is a substantial degree of formal organization. One organizational element, highly decentralized but common to all disciplines, is the academic department. Not every college or university needs to have a separate department devoted to the discipline, but a sizable number must. Moreover, at least a few of these institutions must grant the doctorate or its equivalent for work done in this discipline.

The graduate departments are so influential that they require special attention. For one thing, they serve as gatekeepers to the disciplines. The admission of applicants to graduate school is normally a departmental decision in practice if not in theory, and the student who wishes to enter a discipline can do so only if a department flags him through.

Another task performed by the graduate departments is that of inculcating students with the knowledge and attitudes necessary for playing the professional's role. Universities have granted to their graduate departments sweeping authority for this task. With a few exceptions—such as language requirements, the minimum number of credits that must be taken, the years to be spent in residence, occasional insistence on some work in a second discipline, and the submission of a doctoral dissertation on paper of approved size, weight, and texture—each department is given virtual carte blanche in the preparation of its Ph.D.'s.

Although all graduate departments seem to socialize students in essentially the same fashion and impose much the same requirements, the particular department at which a student takes his doctorate matters a great deal. The source of a man's doctorate is a status symbol that tends to mark him for life. What this means for the discipline in terms of the talent at its disposal and for the individual in terms of where, if not how, he will earn his living we discuss in Chapters 4 and 5.

In addition to the academic departments, learned disciplines have other elements of organization. These typically include a national association and national officers, a central staff, one or more professional journals, and periodic formal meetings of the membership. To the general membership, the journals and the meetings are the more visible.

The journals—one of which is often the official organ of the discipline and as such particularly influential—seek to keep the members informed about research findings and intellectual currents in the profession, as well as with news about personnel, events of current interest, and book reviews. In publishing articles, the journals do more than provide a channel of communication, for publication also serves to legitimize the research reported by certifying that the investigation falls within the scope of the discipline, employs methods acceptable to it, and is not trivial by accepted standards. Conversely, when the journals refuse to publish a person's research findings, they cast doubt on the legitimacy of his work. These and related themes are pursued in Chapter 9, which is devoted to the professional journals in political science, and in Chapter 8, which deals with the factors deemed most important in contributing to professional advancement.

To some extent, the periodic meetings of the membership share with the journals the role of professional validation, for one purpose of these meetings is to provide a forum where research findings can be described and evaluated. Presenting a paper and, to a lesser extent, serving as a discussant or resource person also certify acceptance and legitimacy.

Apart from providing the members with opportunities for extending their network of personal communications (another factor on which career advancement seems to turn), the annual meetings serve another professional function. They provide the occasion for transacting the official business of the discipline. This business normally includes the election of officers and central office staff and the setting of major policy lines. These decisions are usually made at sparsely attended business sessions which rarely do more than ratify, with impressive unanimity, nominations and recommendations made by the incumbent officers and staff.

The officers and staff not only initiate and recommend policies, but, once approved, they also implement them. Many activities supervised by the officers and carried out by the staff are entirely routine—handling of membership matters and publicity releases, arranging for meetings of the membership, and representing the discipline in a variety of interdisciplinary, academic, governmental, and community matters. But officers and staff may do much more. They may, for example, take an active hand in setting editorial policy for the discipline's professional journals, in deciding on the program content of the meetings of the membership, in arranging for and managing various internship and training programs, in allocating research funds at the disposal of the discipline, and in initiating and overseeing the conduct of special research projects undertaken by or in behalf of the discipline.

The members of a discipline who are especially influential in setting the tone and standards of a profession through their control over the apparatus of the central office and of the professional journals and programs and who are likely to have a voice in key appointments are commonly referred to as "the Establishment." The extent to which political scientists believe their discipline is dominated by such an inner circle and the implications of this belief are considered in Chapter 10.

Great Men

Also characteristic of a learned discipline is its gallery of great men—the Michaelsons, Fermis, and Heisenbergs in physics; the Durkheims, Webers, and Sumners in sociology; the Marshalls,

Mitchells, Schumpeters in economics; the Darwins, Pasteurs, and Mendels in biology; the Turners, Taines, Namiers, and Beards in history; the Freuds, Pavlovs, Jameses, and Thurstones in psychology; and the Cantors and Gödels in mathematics. Recognition of greatness normally comes first from within the discipline, although, as Bernard Barber has so well shown, a discipline may be slow and reluctant to accept shattering innovation.[1] In fact, innovators and iconoclasts may receive so little recognition that they are driven from their disciplines altogether.

The Establishment in any discipline may and probably does include some of the discipline's living greats. But it is by no means necessary that this be the case. In either event, there would be much to be gained in seeking to determine which people are held in particular esteem both currently and for earlier contributions. These evaluations of greatness permit inferences not only about those judged, but also about their judges. In Chapter 7 we discuss whom political scientists nominate for their hall of fame and what this tells us about the discipline and its membership.

FUNCTIONS OF A LEARNED DISCIPLINE

One other aspect of a learned discipline concerns us here—the type of functions it typically performs. It is generally agreed that all learned disciplines serve two principal types of functions: (1) teaching—that is, transmitting established knowledge and expertise by lectures, scholarly writing, textbooks, and occasional popular commentary and (2) research. Since our immediate concern at this point is with the graduate department as the socializing instrument of the discipline, we will limit our remarks here to a few trends which relate primarily to the first function.

Although the discipline's transmittal of established knowledge through teaching and writing has long been almost completely associated with educational institutions, only in recent years has the

[1] Bernard Barber, "Resistance by Scientists to Scientific Discovery," in Bernard Barber and Walter Hirsch, eds., *The Sociology of Science* (New York: Free Press of Glencoe, 1963), pp. 539–556.

college and university campus come to be seriously regarded as an exclusive preserve of the Ph.D. This professionalization of the academic community in the sense that it has increasingly come to be dominated by those holding earned doctorates has been one of the most important developments in the learned disciplines.

The precise extent to which this has occurred is not entirely clear from the available data. As Harold Orlans has pointed out, the most relevant of these data—those collected by the National Education Association—are of doubtful validity.[2] Nor are we prepared to draw firm inferences about other disciplines from the data we have compiled about political science. Still, developments in our own profession are suggestive. Teaching members of the American Political Science Association with Ph.D.'s jumped from just under 50 per cent in 1948 to slightly more than 75 per cent in 1961. Even these figures understate the degree of professionalization. If only those holding professorial rank (that is, assistant, associate, and full) are counted, some 80 per cent of the political scientists teaching at American colleges and universities in 1961 held a doctor's degree. Thus, the first commandment in the academic decalogue, "Thou shalt have a doctorate," is, at least for political science, far more honored in the practice than in the breach.

A major, if not the controlling, reason for this trend is the well-documented desire of academic administrators to staff their faculties with as large a proportion of Ph.D.'s as possible, since this figure, like the number of books in the institution's library and the Scholastic Aptitude scores of its freshman class, is almost universally treated as a surrogate of quality. Such a situation poses, of course, serious career problems for the academic who does not have—nor is likely ever to get—his degree. These problems are explored in Chapter 11.

Those of us in certain of the social sciences and, even more so, in the humanities tend to assume that the overwhelming majority of Ph.D.'s earn their living in academic institutions. This is not the case. Only 40 per cent of the Ph.D.'s in the physical sciences and 60 per cent in the biological sciences serve in educational institu-

[2] Harold Orlans, *The Effects of Federal Programs on Higher Education* (Washington, D.C.: Brookings Institution, 1962), p. 13.

tions. Furthermore, increasing numbers of economists and psychologists are going into government and industry rather than into teaching. As Bernard Berelson has recently observed, du Pont employs more Ph.D.'s than Harvard or Yale; General Electric, more than twice as many as Princeton; and the federal government, more than the top ten universities put together.[3]

Still, this trend has not taken place in every learned discipline. It has largely left the humanities untouched, and, in the social sciences, political science and sociology seem also to be exceptions. The proportion of sociologists in academic life, about 75 per cent, has remained fairly constant for the past two decades,[4] whereas that of political scientists has actually increased from 60 per cent in 1953 to better than 70 per cent in 1961.[5] The fact that a decreasing percentage of our profession is outside the academic community raises some interesting questions. Do the attitudes of academics and nonacademics differ? If so, how? And with what possible consequences for the discipline as a whole? Answers to these questions are sought in Chapter 11, which focuses on the two have-not minorities in the profession, the nonacademic and the academic who lacks a doctorate.

A closing comment on the data used in this volume. Although there has been a deluge of recent writing on the state of American political science, virtually all of it has been impressionistic and speculative. In contrast, much of the material on which this book relies is derived from responses to questionnaires sent to a systematic sample of American political scientists. For the interest of the more technically minded, occasional brief methodological notes appear at appropriate places in the text. We have also attached a short appendix on the construction of the questionnaire and on the factor-

[3] Bernard Berelson, *Graduate Education in the United States* (New York: McGraw-Hill Book Co., Inc., 1960), p. 56.

[4] Elbridge Sibley, *The Education of Sociologists in the United States* (New York: Russell Sage Foundation, 1963), p. 47.

[5] Based on an analysis of Franklin L. Burdette, ed., *Biographical Directory of the American Political Science Association* (4th ed.; Washington, D.C.: American Political Science Association, 1961). Hereafter this will be referred to as *Directory*.

analytic techniques and sampling methods used (see Appendix A). Although the issue is treated at greater length in Appendix A, we think it is essential to stress here our conviction that the several hundred replies received reflect with reasonable accuracy present thinking in the profession.

The data produced by several hundred replies make it possible to examine in meaningful terms the views of American political scientists on a broad range of intellectual and professional issues currently facing their discipline. In this way we attempt to add, in each of the chapters that follow, something to the present skimpy knowledge about these matters. But we are well aware that, in seeking to do this, we have more often than not answered fewer questions than we have posed. Moreover, as this introduction implies and as Appendix C also points up explicitly and in detail, there are many questions which, for want of relevant evidence, we do not even raise in the body of the book. For, although the questions begging consideration are very numerous, hard data with which to answer them are generally both fugitive and episodic. Still, not everything can be done at once, and one must start somewhere.

-2-

The State of the Discipline: Consensus or Conflict?

If a learned discipline is to flourish, some intellectual disagreement is necessary. Scientific inquiry is often encouraged and stimulated when probing questions and disconcerting doubts are raised about the wisdom of the *status quo*. At the same time, a certain amount of consensus is essential lest the discord end not in progress but in tearing the discipline apart.

In the past few years political science has enjoyed an abundance of literature dealing with the state of the discipline. However these books and articles differ in other respects, all of them center on a recurring series of questions: What are the principal sources of discord? What major issues are, or should be, facing the profession? What are the merits of the competing viewpoints?

Much of this literature is worth reading. The authors are highly knowledgeable, their analyses shrewd and perceptive, and their insights most suggestive. But almost without exception these writers are subject to a common shortcoming—they rely largely on their own intuition and offhand personal observations both in identifying the big issues and in gauging the intellectual inclinations and commitments of the discipline's membership. This does not mean that those who have written on the state of the discipline are necessarily wrong—or right. It does mean that their conclusions have been almost independent of systematically developed supporting evidence.

We became increasingly convinced, as we combed this literature, that any meaningful discussion of the profession's views on major issues would have to be based on more and harder evidence than was hitherto available. In structuring this study of American political science, we accordingly devoted a substantial portion (the twenty-six statements in Part B of the questionnaire) specifically to this task. The resulting data make it possible to speak with reasonable certitude about where American political scientists stand on the professional issues presumed to divide them. Since our conclusions in this area rest, in the final analysis, on responses to Part B of the questionnaire, it is essential that the reader understand the procedures followed in selecting these twenty-six statements.

When considering how to ascertain the views of the profession on the questions currently confronting political science, we were presented with two options. We could formulate a series of statements which, in our judgment, adequately covered the major issues of the day, or we could take verbatim or paraphrase actual statements from the current literature—statements which, in the opinion of their authors, dealt with topics of urgent concern to political scientists. Either set of statements—ours or those derived from the writings of others—could then be embodied in the questionnaire and used to measure the attitudes of the profession. The great merit of the latter course was that it would systematically exploit the collective wisdom and insights of other recent commentators rather than simply reflect our own notions, however inspired. Consequently, we chose this alternative.

Naturally, judgment had to be exercised in deciding which of the many available statements to use. To reduce the likelihood that significant topics had been overlooked, a pretest version of the entire questionnaire, which covered a number of subjects besides these issues, was sent to a panel of some seventy people. The panel was stratified to include political scientists in both academic and non-academic employment, those at graduate and at undergraduate institutions, persons identified with the several different fields of specialization, and representatives of various age groups. The pretest panel members proved generous with their time and thought. They responded with some lengthy and detailed critiques of the undertaking itself and of the various sections of the questionnaire. By and large, the statements in Part B stood up rather well, although the panelists pointed to one topic that we had missed altogether, to a couple of statements that could well be dropped, and to others that would profit from minor rewording. Many of these suggestions were incorporated in the final version of the questionnaire.

Thus, although the ultimate responsibility for the final selection is ours alone, the decision that the twenty-six propositions finally incorporated in Part B adequately reflect the issues raised in the more recent literature was one on which we had the advice of a substantial number of other political scientists. Of course, we subsequently received many additional comments from the larger body of respondents. Although criticisms were by no means infrequent and, in some instances, acidulous, there was general agreement that we had pretty well covered the leading problems of the day.[1]

---

[1] We quote: "The likes of this questionnaire may be part of what is 'wrong' with current political science." "Precisely the sort of questionnaire and research technique that irritates political scientists who feel that the behaviorists are prisoners of their own primitive methodology." "These are ridiculous questions and I decline to attempt to answer them. Sorry." "Frankly, I am extremely irritated by your damn foolish questions." "I have little faith in questionnaires." "I doubt the validity of the question and the literacy of the questioner." "I think my answers are about as meaningless as your questions." "Your questionnaire is geared to the 'profession' as constituted—aimless, arrogant, preoccupied with inflated secondary problems." There were, of course, the more perceptive respondents: "It's a good questionnaire. I look forward to hearing your results." "It's quite a decent questionnaire even though a little transparent in spots." "An excellent questionnaire."

RESPONSES TO INDIVIDUAL STATEMENTS

The position taken by a respondent on any issue or statement is to some degree a function of the choice of possible answers. For purposes of this inquiry, a five-point Likert-type scale—"strongly agree," "agree," "can't say," "disagree," "strongly disagree"—seemed to afford a practicable and adequately discriminating range of responses. The following table summarizes the position taken by 431 respondents on each of the twenty-six "intellectual issues" items.[2] All figures are given in percentages.

Item 1, for example, states, "Much that passes for scholarship in political science is superficial and trivial." The answers ran from 17 per cent on "strongly agree" to 2 per cent on "strongly disagree." In one respect, the responses to this item are typical. With few exceptions, the replies run heavily to the moderate ("agree" or "disagree") rather than to the extreme ("strongly agree" or "strongly disagree") positions. Only once did the frequency of strong responses reach the 45 per cent mark (Item 25); on Item 4 it hit 28.7 per cent, and on the majority of the others it was well below the 20 per cent level. By and large, two-thirds of the judgments expressed fell into one of the moderate categories.

Another general characteristic (here Item 1 is definitely atypical) was the substantial incidence of "can't say" responses. The statements presented for evaluation deal with problems presumed to be of pressing intellectual concern to the profession. Nevertheless, "can't say" responses ranged from a low of 3.2 per cent (Item 25) to a high of 45.9 (Item 26), with a mean score of 15.9 per cent, or almost one in six. The disinclination to take a stand may spring from lack of interest, lack of knowledge, or indecision about the merits of the matter. However, when this characteristic is added to that noted above, the following generalization seems warranted: To

[2] Questionnaires were sent to every fifth member of the American Political Science Association listed in the 1961 *Directory* (full-time students excluded). About twenty-five returned questionnaires could not be used because of insufficient data; another twenty or so were returned too late to be included in our analysis.

TABLE 1

POSITION OF PROFESSION ON INTELLECTUAL ISSUES

Item

1. Much that passes for scholarship in political science is superficial or trivial.

2. Political scientists in the United States are unhappy about the current state of their discipline.

3. Political science cannot be said to have any generally agreed upon body of methods and techniques.

4. Much research in political science is undertaken simply because the projects lend themselves to research by a fashionable tool or because financial support can readily be secured.

5. By and large, the preparation of a doctoral dissertation in political science is not an intellectually satisfying experience.

6. The *American Political Science Review* currently devotes an unduly large amount of space to materials reflecting a behavioral approach.

7. Communication among political scientists tends to be seriously hindered by the inadequacy of their basic concepts.

8. Political scientists tend to be unsophisticated about the nature of scientific investigation.

9. Efforts to formulate, refine, and clarify concepts and to obtain agreement on labels to be attached to concepts often result in little more than hairsplitting and jargon.

10. The articles currently being published in the *APSR* are of a generally better quality than those published before World War II.

11. The involvement of political scientists in nonscholarly activities has tended to impede the development of the discipline.

12. A substantial part of the intellectual conflict in American political science is rooted in issues that are methodological in character.

13. Doctoral programs in political science stress research training at the cost of preparing effective undergraduate teachers.

		Response		
Strongly agree	Agree	Can't say	Disagree	Strongly disagree
17.4%	48.3%	5.1%	27.1%	2.1%
8.6	46.2	25.1	18.6	1.6
18.3	48.3	3.7	27.4	2.3
27.8	44.8	9.5	16.9	.9
6.0	24.6	19.5	41.1	8.8
15.8	28.8	7.2	34.1	14.2
11.1	37.6	11.6	38.1	1.6
8.8	38.2	9.0	40.4	3.5
14.8	48.0	5.6	28.5	3.0
10.2	28.3	45.2	13.9	2.3
3.9	14.4	18.3	47.8	15.5
4.9	16.5	12.5	54.5	11.6
17.2	39.4	13.9	25.1	4.4

TABLE 1 (*Continued*)

POSITION OF PROFESSION ON INTELLECTUAL ISSUES

Item

14. The mood of contemporary American political science is one of stock-taking and self-criticism.

15. Given the present state of political science, efforts to develop a general theory of politics are premature.

16. American political science has developed an Establishment which largely determines the character and standards of the discipline.

17. A high proportion of political scientists actually think of themselves as scientists only in a broad and figurative sense.

18. Doctoral programs in political science stress techniques rather than broad understanding and cultivation.

19. By and large, political scientists do not devote enough attention to contemporary public policy matters.

20. Political science has generally competed rather successfully with the other social sciences in areas of common interest and study.

21. Political scientists seem not to engage in studies in which it is possible for one investigator to replicate the findings of another.

22. Much of the work being done in political behavior is only marginally related to political science.

23. The really significant problems of political life cannot be successfully attacked by the behavioral approach.

24. The American political scientist has in recent years become increasingly concerned with the adequacy of his methodology.

25. Every doctoral candidate in political science should have systematic training in the history of political thought.

26. There has developed an inner group in the American Political Science Association which, in large part, controls the key panel assignments at the annual Association meetings.

		Response		
Strongly agree	Agree	Can't say	Disagree	Strongly disagree
10.0%	50.1%	19.7%	18.3%	1.9%
10.7	27.1	8.4	40.1	13.1
10.0	36.0	25.3	26.7	2.1
16.5	64.0	13.5	5.5	.5
9.7	29.0	21.3	37.1	2.8
7.7	26.9	9.7	47.3	8.4
5.1	45.7	17.6	27.8	3.7
5.3	38.2	24.8	29.0	2.6
19.0	21.8	10.9	36.0	12.3
14.4	24.1	15.8	31.8	13.9
18.6	66.1	10.2	4.9	.2
47.1	36.4	3.2	10.4	2.8
14.4	27.6	45.9	10.2	1.9

a rather surprising degree, American political scientists do not take
a position on these issues; on the other hand, they seem not to be
very firmly committed on the positions they do take. This is a
phenomenon which we will subsequently discuss in more sober detail.

ALTERNATIVE MODES OF ANALYSIS

It is possible to handle the data in Table 1 in three ways.
First, one can study the over-all responses to the individual statements in order to determine where the profession stands on each
of these topics. Take Item 11, for example, which bears on an issue
which has concerned Charles Hyneman, among others.[3] Do political
scientists really think that involvement in politics, government service, and other nonscholarly pursuits has impeded the development
of the discipline? Or Item 25—does the membership feel that systematic training in the history of political thought is a systematic
waste of time? Or, as a last illustration, Items 5, 13, and 18. How
do political scientists assess their system of doctoral training? Are
their views similar to those of persons in the physical and biological sciences? Something of an answer to both questions can be
obtained by comparing the responses to these statements with the
data on the adequacy of doctoral programs presented by Berelson
in his study of graduate schools.[4] Different people will, of course, be
interested in different problems, and this type of analysis, which
really requires little exposition by us, can for the most part be left
to the reader himself.

A second mode of analysis is also used in the chapters that
follow. This method is multivariate in the sense that we attempt
to determine whether subgroups in the profession—that is, people
in different fields, with diverse Ph.D. origins, or with opposing views
—differ in their responses to discrete items among the twenty-six

[3] *The Study of Politics* (Urbana, Ill.: University of Illinois Press,
1958), Chap. I.
[4] *Op. cit.*, pp. 156–215.

statements. We will apply this and, on occasion, the first technique in dealing with data from Part B of the questionnaire.

But we can also analyze the twenty-six items in a third way, one that is multivariate in another sense. In this approach an effort is made to reduce the larger body of statements to a smaller number of truly basic issues. For this purpose we used factor analysis, with results that turned out to be analytically very useful because they enabled us to deal with the views of the entire profession and its major subgroups on these underlying issues.

The factors which emerged have sufficient explanatory power to warrant a full discussion. The next chapter, accordingly, deals with the basic issues identified by factor analysis. In discussing these issues, we will attempt to give the nontechnician some notion of what we have done. Readers interested in the statistical procedures will find them in Appendix A.

-3-

The Key Issues

The eleven thousand odd answers to the twenty-six statements were reduced to a smaller number of statistically independent underlying components or factors, and the extent to which each statement associated with each factor was ascertained. An IBM 7094 computer faithfully assisted in this otherwise impossibly tedious task. We then examined the statements most strongly associated with each factor in the hope that they would suggest an intuitively meaningful name for the factor.

This mode of analysis produced two large and stable factors. One of these accounted for almost 40 per cent of the variance in the responses to the twenty-six statements; the other, for 20 per cent.[1] To draw an analogy to a statistic with which the general

---

[1] Squared multiple correlations were used as the estimate of communality.

reader may be more familiar, it would take a multiple correlation greater than .75 to account for this much variance. Each of the two major factors seemed, in our opinion, to identify a key current issue.

Behavioralism

An examination of the extent to which each of the twenty-six statements associated with the larger of the two factors disclosed that three in particular correlate with it strongly. In order of magnitude, they are:

23. The really significant problems of political life cannot be successfully attacked by the behavioral approach.
22. Much of the work being done in political behavior is only marginally related to political science.
6. The *American Political Science Review* currently devotes an unduly large amount of space to materials reflecting a behavioral approach.

Even a casual inspection of the wording of these propositions leaves no doubt that this factor may be labeled "behavioralism." Other statements (Items 9 and 10) associated with the factor to a lesser, though still highly significant, degree confirm the appropriateness of behavioralism as the name for this single most important factor.

To find that political scientists consider behavioralism the single most important issue facing the discipline may seem a totally unnecessary demonstration of the obvious. Connoisseurs of the professional literature hardly require a survey to tell them that the behavioral controversy has flooded political science journals for more than a decade. Be that as it may, there are at least two other no less weighty questions with which this survey enables us to deal: How are attitudes toward behavioralism distributed? What other values and beliefs are correlated with attitudes toward it?

The answers to these questions require, in turn, some sort of scale with which to measure attitudes toward behavioralism. This task is not without its problems, since the one point on which leading commentators do agree is that there is little agreement on the precise meaning of the term. Here again, factor analysis proved useful. With it we were able to construct an operational measure of behavioralism. Although the procedural details can be of interest only to the technician and have, accordingly, been relegated to Appendix A, what we did in general was to compute a behavioralism factor score for each respondent. This score was based on a combination of two sets of weights: (1) the individual's answers to the five questions most highly associated with the behavioral factor and (2) the more than eleven thousand answers provided by all respondents to the twenty-six statements.

After converting the raw factor scores into scores (we used a mean of fifty and standard deviation of ten) that would facilitate subsequent comparative analysis, we were able to scale the position of the entire body of respondents on the issue of behavioralism. Chart 1 shows how the attitudes of American political scientists toward behavioralism are distributed.

Several inferences may be drawn from this chart. For one thing, American political scientists have certainly not reached anything like consensus on behavioralism. If there were consensus, the distribution would have tended to be unimodal. In other words, a very large proportion of the respondents to the questionnaire would have been concentrated in a very narrow score range. But, although the discipline has not attained consensus, neither is it divided into two distinct, opposing camps which threaten to tear it apart. If this were the case, the distribution would have tended to be bimodal. That is, substantial proportions of the respondents would have been concentrated at two widely separated points on the scale.

Although the distribution reveals neither consensus nor sharp conflict, it certainly is not the kind of normal bell-shaped distribution so familiar from height and weight charts, intelligence tests, and College Board SAT scores. If this were the case, scores between 40 and 60—that is, plus or minus one standard deviation—would have constituted only about one-third of the range of scale scores. On the behavioral factor scale, however, scores between 40 and 60 comprise 48.3 per cent of the total range of scores.

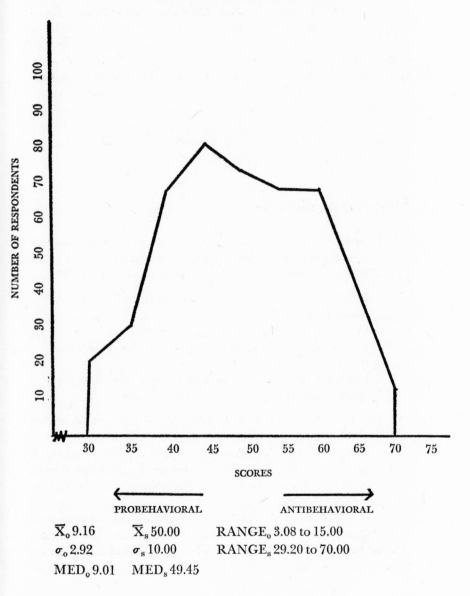

CHART 1

DISTRIBUTION OF AMERICAN POLITICAL SCIENTISTS
ON THE BEHAVIORAL FACTOR

$\overline{X}_o$ 9.16 $\overline{X}_s$ 50.00 $RANGE_o$ 3.08 to 15.00
σ_o 2.92 σ_s 10.00 $RANGE_s$ 29.20 to 70.00
MED_o 9.01 MED_s 49.45

What Chart 1 does show is a distribution of behavioralism scores that is more-or-less rectangular, or platykurtic. This strongly suggests that there is a continuum of attitudes toward behavioralism with sizable support along most of the continuum. At no point is there an especially heavy concentration of respondents, and only at the outer range of scores does support drop off fairly sharply. Still, even the extremes get some support, with extremists of both sides comprising perhaps 20 to 25 per cent of the discipline. Moreover, the close juxtaposition of the mean, the median, and the mid-point of the range of possible scores indicates that the profession is about equally divided between those who are at least somewhat behaviorally oriented and those who are not.

Adequacy of the Profession

The second most important factor accounted for approximately 20 per cent of the total variance. Three statements are strongly correlated with this second factor. Again, in order of magnitude:

8. Political scientists tend to be unsophisticated about the nature of scientific investigation.
7. Communication among political scientists tends to be seriously hindered by the inadequacy of their basic concepts.
3. Political science cannot be said to have any generally agreed upon body of methods and techniques.

This factor we have named "adequacy of the profession" because we think that agreement with the three statements reveals a feeling that political science is not now able to cope effectively with its problems as a learned discipline, whereas disagreement reflects the belief that it can and is doing so. No other statements strongly correlate with this factor.

It is extremely important to remember that the behavioralism and adequacy factors are independent of one another. The attitudes expressed about behavioralism are not to any appreciable degree related to opinions on the adequacy of the discipline. Persons sympathetic to behavioralism are no more likely to consider the discipline adequate (or inadequate) than are the antibehavioralists.

Adequacy factor scores were computed for each respondent in the same manner used to compute scores for the behavioral factor. The distribution of adequacy scores has been plotted on Chart 2, together with the behavioral factor scores.

The similarity in the distribution on the two factors is strikingly apparent. Both are platykurtic. Attitudes toward the adequacy of the discipline, like those toward behavioralism, find substantial support along most of the score range, without a heavy concentration in any narrow segment. However, one difference should be noted. The mean and the median of the adequacy distribution fall at about 50.0, whereas the mid-point of the entire range of possible—and, in this instance, actual—scores is at 47.4. Apparently, those who regard the discipline as at least somewhat inadequate comprise a small majority of all respondents.

Stability of Two Key Factors

Another similarity between the behavioralism and adequacy factors, which together account for 60 per cent of the variance in the answers to the twenty-six statements, is particularly impressive. Both factors are persistent and stable. On almost every one of the several dozen analyses we ran on subgroups of respondents, behavioralism and adequacy were both present and large. As one might expect when two factors account for such a large share of the variance in a set of answers, respondents' scores on the behavioralism and adequacy factors and their replies to other sections of the questionnaire are related. In fact, the relationships are so numerous and so substantial that they will be treated in most subsequent chapters.

Only one other factor showed anything like the stability of behavioralism and adequacy. It accounts for 7 per cent of the variance in the answers of all respondents to the twenty-six statements and deals with the existence of a powerful Establishment in political science, a subject examined at some length in Chapter 10. Other

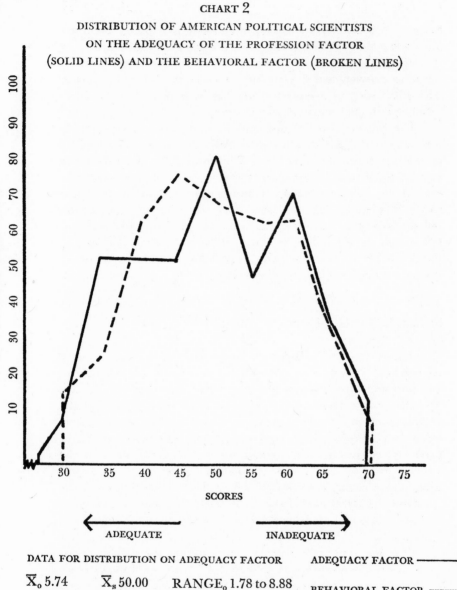

CHART 2

DISTRIBUTION OF AMERICAN POLITICAL SCIENTISTS
ON THE ADEQUACY OF THE PROFESSION FACTOR
(SOLID LINES) AND THE BEHAVIORAL FACTOR (BROKEN LINES)

DATA FOR DISTRIBUTION ON ADEQUACY FACTOR   ADEQUACY FACTOR ————

$\overline{X}_o$ 5.74 $\overline{X}_s$ 50.00   RANGE$_o$ 1.78 to 8.88   BEHAVIORAL FACTOR ----------
σ_o 1.58 σ_s 10.00   RANGE$_s$ 25.00 to 69.86
MED$_o$ 5.75   MED$_s$ 50.08

factors did not prove stable enough to be analytically useful and consequently will not be discussed in this book.

To recapitulate the foregoing discussion: American political scientists, factor analysis indicates, are divided by two major but independent issues. The larger of these is behavioralism, the smaller we have called "adequacy of the profession." Although these are currently the two big questions, they do not seem to polarize the profession, nor does a large proportion of our membership take a strong or extremist position on either of them. The implications of this type of opinion distribution and the relationship between views on these two factors, on the one hand, and perceptions and values on a variety of other questions of professional importance, on the other, will be explored in greater detail in the pages to come.

-4-

The Prestige Departments

It is simply a "fact of life," declares Bernard Berelson, "that some universities are better than others."[1] A more precise statement would be that some departments are *believed* to be better than others, for there is no infallible method of objectively quantifying the actual quality of schools. But where one deals with qualitative assessments, the relationship of fact to reality is often less important than the existence of the belief and the behavior that results from its acceptance. As W. I. Thomas has said, "If men define situations as real, they are real in their consequences."

It is also a fact of life—for many persons, a very unfortunate fact—that some political science departments are believed to be better than others. In this chapter we will examine (1) the profession's evaluation of the relative quality of graduate political sci-

[1] *Op. cit.*, p. 96.

ence departments, (2) the consequences to the individual and to the discipline of the resulting prestige hierarchy, and (3) the evidence which seems to corroborate or challenge these assumptions of departmental merit. Since professional training in political science as in the other learned disciplines is that directed toward the Ph.D., the discussion will deal only with departments offering work culminating in this degree. The thirty-three institutions represented in our ranking account for the overwhelming preponderance (some 80 per cent) of doctorates in political science.[2]

To appreciate fully the working of the departmental status system, we must consider it against the background of three trends in the discipline over the past fifteen years. Two of these, academization and professionalization, are discussed in Chapter 1. The third, changes in the part played by various departments in producing Ph.D.'s, requires brief comment at this point.

CHANGING PATTERNS OF DOCTORAL OUTPUT

As we all know, there has been a vast increase in the production of Ph.D.'s in political science. Between 1936 and 1942, 493 doctorates were awarded. Over the next seven years, 1943–1949, the figure dropped to 464. Then the floodgates opened. In the next seven years, 1950–1956, 1,289 Ph.D.'s were turned out. Annual output has continued to move upward, going from 201 in 1956–1957 to 238 in 1961–1962, the last year for which complete data are available.[3]

---

[2] Our list is made up of those schools which lead in training political science Ph.D.'s. The University of Southern California and the University of Pittsburgh were omitted because their doctorates are largely limited to public administration; Tufts, because of its emphasis on international relations.

[3] Figures for the periods 1936–1942, 1943–1949, and 1950–1956 are taken from *Doctorate Production in United States Universities 1936–56* (Office of Scientific Personnel, Publication 582) [Washington, D.C.: National Academy of Sciences-National Research Council, 1958]), p. 7. Data for each of the subsequent years are from the annual publication of the Office of Education, U.S. Department of Health, Education, and Welfare, entitled either *Earned Degrees Conferred, Bachelor's and Higher Degrees*

At the same time, there have been some drastic shifts in the contributions to this output by the several graduate departments, as can be seen in Table 2. This table gives the rank order, number, and percentage of total output accounted for by the ten largest departments (in terms of doctoral output) for the first and the last of the periods mentioned above—1936–1942 and 1957–1962. For each of these periods, it should be remembered, these ten are only a relatively small minority of the number of departments awarding doctorates in the discipline.

TABLE 2

LARGEST SOURCES OF DOCTORATES
1936–1942 AND 1957–1962

1957–1962	Rank	%	No.	1936–1942	Rank	%	No.
Columbia	1	8.5	97	Harvard	1	13.6	67
Chicago	2	8.3	95	Chicago	2	9.7	48
Harvard	3	8.2	93	Columbia	3	8.7	43
American	4	5.0	57	Iowa	4	5.7	28
N.Y.U.	5	4.4	50	Princeton	5	5.0	25
Princeton	6	3.8	43	Yale	6	4.1	20
Michigan	7	3.6	41	Wisconsin	7	3.7	18
Yale	8	3.5	40	Illinois	8	3.5	17
Georgetown	9	3.3	38	Calif. (Berk.)	9.5	3.3	16
Indiana	10	3.1	36	N.Y.U.	9.5	3.3	16
Total, top ten		53.5	608	Total, top ten		60.2	297
Total, all schools		100.0	1137	Total, all schools		100.0	493

or *Earned Degrees Conferred by Higher Educational Institutions.* The most recent of these covers the academic year 1961–1962. Totals for 1956 and subsequent years represent the combined output in political science, international relations, and public administration, since these are treated as separate categories in the Office of Education annual compilations. We are indebted to Charles P. Hurd, registrar, Columbia University, and Wayne E. Tolliver of the Office of Education for assistance in providing us with information otherwise not readily available. Comparable data for the other social sciences are given by Sibley, *op. cit.,* p. 45.

Two changes are especially noteworthy. First, there was a decline in the percentage of Ph.D.'s trained at the ten "largest" schools. For decades the "big ten," led by Harvard, Chicago, and Columbia, traditionally produced a substantial majority of political science doctorates, accounting for some 60 per cent in 1936–1942 and nearly 65 per cent in 1943–1949.[4] Early in the 1950's, the pattern began to alter. For 1950–1956, their contribution dropped to 57 per cent; for the next six years, it fell further, to 54 per cent, holding at that point during 1961–1962.[5] This decline in the relative output of the larger departments means, of course, that almost half of the new doctorates are now being awarded by the "smaller" departments.

Concomitantly, the composition of the "big ten" has undergone a substantial transformation. Historically, the largest producers were also the most highly regarded departments. The lion's share of Ph.D.'s traditionally came, then, from departments which were prestigious as well as sizable. But by the early 1960's, as we shall shortly see, at least four of the big departments do not rank among the elite in the profession's status system. What has taken place is thus a twofold revolution—not only are the smaller and less well-known departments granting a larger proportion of doctorates in political science, but also the larger producers now include among their membership several of the less prestigious departments. The consequences of this revolution become apparent when we examine the structure and functioning of our departmental pecking order.

RANKINGS OF DEPARTMENTAL QUALITY

Offhand evaluations of the comparative strength of various departments are constantly made both in fraternal shoptalk—where

[4] For the first time in decades, as far as we can determine, Columbia has moved ahead of both Harvard and Chicago in doctoral output. The inclusion of the 1961–1962 data drops Harvard from first to third place.

[5] Harvard, Columbia, and Chicago accounted for some 35 per cent of the doctorates *in the profession* in the late 1940's—and barely 25 per cent by 1961. These figures are based on degrees reported in the Association's directories for 1948 and 1961. These three schools also accounted for exactly 25 per cent of the new political science Ph.D.'s in 1961–1962.

the subject is second in popularity only to that of desirable staff openings—and in the advising of graduate students. However knowledgeable these casual estimates may be, they are hardly an adequate basis for a formal ranking. Over the decades, therefore, a number of attempts have been made to obtain more systematic and reliable ratings.

In 1925, Raymond M. Hughes, relying on the opinions of nineteen "leading political scientists," ranked the eleven "best" departments (there was a tie for ninth place).[6] Nine years later, Hughes tried again. This time, apparently having learned his lesson, he satisfied himself with identifying the eight "most distinguished departments"—carefully presented in alphabetical order.[7] Hayward Keniston's 1957 rating of the leading fifteen political science departments, part of a study which has since become required reading for academic administrators, was the next attempt and reflected the opinions of twenty-five departmental chairmen.[8] The latest was our own inquiry, undertaken in 1963 and based on responses from a systematic sample of the members of the American Political Science Association.[9]

All such rating efforts, as Keniston pointed out, are subject to serious limitations. "They depend on highly subjective impressions; they reflect old and new loyalties; they are subject to lag, and the halo of past prestige."[10] We would add other limitations. There is a tendency to overrank those institutions with which one has been personally associated, sometimes also called the "halo effect"; further, there is often some question of just what is being ranked—the quality of the faculty, the student body, the course offerings, the research facilities, or any combination of these; and there is the problem of translating qualitative assessments into quantitative scores.

[6] *The Graduate Schools of America* (Oxford, Ohio: Miami University Press, 1925), pp. 22–23.

[7] "Report of the Committee on Graduate Instruction," *The Educational Record*, XV, No. 2 (1934), 220–221.

[8] *Graduate Study and Research in the Arts and Sciences at the University of Pennsylvania* (Philadelphia: University of Pennsylvania Press, 1959), p. 142.

[9] Item C-7, questionnaire, Appendix B-2, p. 159.

[10] *Op. cit.*, p. 117.

Certain of these limitations, such as the subjectivity of the ratings, are inherent in the nature of the undertaking. From our viewpoint, however, this was not all to the bad since we were less concerned with what is actually the situation than with what the profession *believes* to be the case. We attempted to compensate for the other limitations by the way in which the inquiry was worded and by the methods used in analyzing the responses. Respondents were asked to rate the departments in terms of the "over-all quality of the doctoral program" rather than of faculty, students, or courses of study alone. Analysis revealed that there was a slight halo effect in that respondents tended to overrank the institution at which they had taken their doctorates, but the actual rank order of departments was not thereby affected. We experimented with several methods of assigning weights to the various responses. In no instance did a reasonable alternative change the position of a top-listed department by more than one place; in only two cases did it produce a shift of more than a single rank among the departments in the remaining portion of the list.[11]

To facilitate direct comparison with Hughes's awkward 1925 listing of the eleven "best" departments, we employed the same cut-off point in selecting those to be classified as best in the later two rankings (Keniston's and ours). For the purposes of this study, we are utilizing only two categories—"best" schools and "other" schools —although we realize that there may be profound differences of quality as well as prestige among the twenty-two institutions comprising the "other" category. Some readers may also see distinct subcategory possibilities in the eleven top-rated departments. We would tend to agree, but we certainly are not prepared to argue that our scoring technique is sufficiently sensitive and sophisticated to justify these subclassifications on quantitative grounds alone.

The rankings produced by the three studies mentioned above are as follows:

[11] The system finally utilized gave three points for an "excellent," two for a "good," and one for a "fair." "Poor" ratings received zero weight. The total number of points earned was then divided by the total number of evaluations, including "poors," to give a prestige index rating score.

TABLE 3

RANKING OF POLITICAL SCIENCE DEPARTMENTS
1925, 1957, 1963

1925 (Hughes)		1957 (Keniston)		1963 (S-T)		1963 Index score
1	Harvard	1	Harvard	1	Harvard	2.59
2	Chicago	2	Chicago	2	Yale	2.53
3	Columbia	3	Calif. (Berk.)	3	Calif. (Berk.)	2.48
4	Wisconsin	4	Columbia	4	Chicago	2.45
5	Illinois	5	Princeton	5	Princeton	2.32
6	Michigan	6	Michigan	6	Columbia	2.29
7	Princeton	7	Yale	7	Michigan	2.15
8	Johns Hopkins	8	Wisconsin	8.5	Stanford	2.07
9.5	Iowa	9	Minnesota	8.5	Wisconsin	2.07
9.5	Pennsylvania	10	Cornell	10.5	Calif. (U.C.L.A.)	1.97
11	Calif. (Berk.)	11	Illinois	10.5	Cornell	1.97
		12	Calif. (U.C.L.A.)	12	Johns Hopkins	1.93
		13	Stanford	13	Northwestern	1.92
		14	Johns Hopkins	14	Indiana	1.88
		15	Duke	15	Illinois	1.85
				16	Minnesota	1.81
				17	North Carolina	1.77
				18.5	Duke	1.62
				18.5	Syracuse	1.62
				20	Pennsylvania	1.51
				21	Vanderbilt	1.38
				22	N.Y.U.	1.35
				23	Michigan State	1.32
				24.5	Iowa	1.29
				24.5	Ohio State	1.29
				26	Washington (Seattle)	1.24
				27.5	Georgetown	1.10
				27.5	Texas	1.10
				29	American	.858
				30	Notre Dame	.847
				31	George Washington	.824
				32	Fordham	.658
				33	Catholic	.553

The Best Departments: Many Are Called but
Few Are Chosen

The regularity with which the same schools are identified as the best is all the more striking when one considers the diverse techniques by which the three rankings were compiled and the forty-year span they cover. Of the eleven leading departments in 1925, eight retain their place of honor on one or both of the later listings. Both the composition of this elite group and the individual departmental positions are quite consistent. Harvard, perhaps illustrating our earlier comment that belief is often as important as fact, is first on all three ratings. Chicago takes two second places and one fourth; Columbia, a third, fourth, and sixth place; and Princeton two fifth places and a seventh place. The widest move is made by Berkeley, which rose from eleventh place in 1925 to third in the 1957 and 1963 compilations. Once having achieved eminence, a department seems almost to acquire a form of tenure, with only three of the original eleven schools falling entirely from grace between 1925 and 1963.

This stability, however gratifying to the departments which have arrived, is simultaneously a major cause of frustration to those attempting to gain recognition. We all know of the energy, labor, thought, and even money expended at a number of institutions in quest of prestige status. Yet, in four decades, only two departments, Cornell and Yale, not listed in 1925 moved into this select company on both of the later rankings. Only three, Minnesota on Keniston's and Stanford and U.C.L.A. on ours, managed to make it on one or the other.

What factors seem related to success or failure in this effort? Expansion of doctoral output alone seems to be of slight, if any, value. In fact, the collective Ph.D. production of the eleven best departments has dropped from 60 per cent of the doctorates granted during 1943–1949 to a relatively modest 48 per cent by 1961–1962. Moreover, four of the ten departments (Table 2) which lead in doctoral output do not appear among the prestige institutions; of the five that did break into one or both of the later rankings, only Yale is a major doctoral source.

A necessary if not a sufficient condition of success is that the aspiring department be a component of a university which is itself prestigious. Keniston ranked graduate schools as well as departments in 1957.[12] All five of the departments which made the transition to best status are at institutions which did well on his ranking, with the lowest placing no worse than fourteenth nationally. The top departments, then, are at the best universities; departments at less prestigious institutions have great difficulty in achieving independent distinction, at least in political science. Clearly, this intimate relationship between institutional ranking and departmental image poses some massive problems for the chairman who sets out to have his department recognized as one of the best.[13]

The "Other" Departments

Any cutoff point for best, whether one picks fifth, tenth, or eleventh as the magic rank, is essentially arbitrary. Exigencies of comparability compelled us to draw the line between eleventh and twelfth place although only .04 of a point separates these two departments. In fact, some of the lower positioned of the "best" departments are closer in prestige index score to the "other" departments than they are to those heading their own category. And, for what solace it affords, there are noteworthy gaps in score and, presumably, in prestige between those at the top and at the bottom, respectively, of this second group.

Throughout this category, we see again a close correlation between departmental and institutional status. For example, Johns Hopkins is sixteenth on Keniston's university ranking, Northwestern seventeenth, Indiana fifteenth, Minnesota twelfth, and Illinois tenth. Five institutions—Duke, Syracuse, Vanderbilt, Michigan State, and Iowa—do not make Keniston's twenty-place listing.

[12] *Op. cit.,* p. 119.
[13] Orlans writes of the parallel "difficulty and expense" of lifting a university to the "topmost national rank." *Op. cit.,* p. 18.

For Ohio State, New York University, and Washington, however, departmental ranking also generally coincides with that of the school. The major exception is Pennsylvania, twentieth in departmental status but eleventh on university position.

If we split the "other" departments into halves, we get a roughly inverse correlation between rank and doctoral output. Only one of the schools in the upper half is a leading source of Ph.D.'s, but three of those in the lower half are. It is possible that the expansion of doctoral output at a school is akin to the acquisition of wealth in a family, requiring the passage of a generation or two to remove the taint of recency and to prepare the way for acceptance in better circles.

There are a number of other characteristics common to the institutions at the lower end of the scale. Four of them—Georgetown, American University, George Washington, and Catholic University—are in the Washington, D.C., area, and are generally believed to have large contingents of part-time doctoral candidates and a comparatively large percentage of Ph.D.'s who do not go into academic work. These beliefs may partially explain the rankings received.

One last, rather touchy note. Three of the four lowest and four of the bottom eight departments are at Catholic institutions. Catholic educators themselves are well aware and have written both perceptively and critically of the difficulties of providing quality graduate education in a denominational institution.[14]

Variables Influencing Ratings of Departments

Although most graduate departments make an effort to provide their students with at least an exposure to the various approaches to political science, some are identified with a partiality or commitment to a particular point of view or school. Yale and Northwestern, for example, are commonly said to be behaviorally oriented, whereas Harvard and Columbia are thought to be more traditional in approach. Is there some relation between the stand persons take

[14] An excellent recent analysis is Edward Wakin's *The Catholic Campus* (New York: Macmillan Co., 1963).

on the behavioralism and adequacy of the profession factors and the way in which they rate departments?

An initial screening revealed that the linear correlations between the two major factors and the responses to most sections of the questionnaire tend to be rather weak. But, when the responses of persons with very high factor scores are compared with the responses of persons with very low factor scores, the differences are more noteworthy. In order to preclude the biases inherent in selecting extreme groups in an *ad hoc* way, we decided to define them in an impersonal and conventional, though admittedly still arbitrary, fashion—the standard deviation. In this chapter and in several that follow, extreme behavioralists are defined as those falling more than one standard deviation below the mean on the behavioral scale; the extreme antibehavioralists are those with scores falling more than one standard deviation above the mean. This places about one-sixth of the respondents in each group (or, more exactly, 38 per cent of the respondents in both groups combined). The same procedure was used in determining the extreme groups in regard to the adequacy factor.

Table 4 shows how the eleven prestige departments are ranked by the extreme groups on the behavioralism and adequacy factor scales.

Both consensus and conflict are clearly indicated. Behavioralists and antibehavioralists find little to quarrel about on six of the eleven departments—Berkeley, Chicago, Princeton, Michigan, Stanford, U.C.L.A., and Cornell—and no more than two ranks separate the evaluations of the two groups. On the other hand, Yale and Wisconsin are sources of severe disagreement, with Harvard and Columbia somewhat less so. When the entire array of behavioral and antibehavioral rankings is compared statistically, the differences in outlook are just substantial enough to warrant the conclusion that they should not be attributed to chance.

The rankings in Table 4 ignore all but the top eleven departments. If the list is extended to include all the departments identified in Table 3, other interesting differences are revealed. The probehavioralists rank Northwestern fifth, Harvard seventh, Indiana eleventh, North Carolina twelfth, Cornell in a tie for fourteenth,

TABLE 4

RANKING OF ELEVEN PRESTIGE POLITICAL SCIENCE DEPARTMENTS
BY RESPONDENTS HAVING EXTREME* SCORES ON BEHAVIORALISM
AND ADEQUACY FACTORS

Department Ranking by all respondents in parenthesis	Behavioralism		Adequacy	
	Anti	Pro	More	Less
Harvard (1)	2	6	3	1
Yale (2)	6	1	2	2
Calif. (Berk.) (3)	3	4	1	3
Chicago (4)	1	2	4	5
Princeton (5)	4	5	5	4
Columbia (6)	5	8	8	6
Michigan (7)	7.5	7	6.5	7
Stanford (8.5)	7.5	9	6.5	9
Wisconsin (8.5)	9	3	10	8
Calif. (U.C.L.A.) (10.5)	11	10	9	10
Cornell (10.5)	10	11	11	11

Tau $=$ .45   Tau $=$ .29
Z $=$ 1.96   Z $=$ 1.26
P (Ho) $<$ .05   P (Ho) $>$ .05

* More extreme than plus or minus one standard deviation.

and Johns Hopkins in a tie for seventeenth. Antibehavioralists, how-ever, rank Johns Hopkins ninth, North Carolina eighteenth, and Northwestern twentieth.

In contrast, the two extreme groups on the adequacy factor view the top eleven schools in much the same manner. No more than two ranks divide them on *any* of the eleven prestige depart-ments. Conflict becomes visible, though, when all departmental ratings are included. Those who regard the discipline as inadequate rank Northwestern sixth, Indiana tenth, and Johns Hopkins in a tie for sixteenth, whereas those who find it more adequate place Johns Hopkins eleventh, Indiana in a tie for fourteenth, and North-western sixteenth.

The extent to which perceptions of departmental excellence are

TABLE 5

RANK ORDER RATINGS OF TOP ELEVEN DEPARTMENTS BY FIELD OF RESPONDENTS

	Over-all	Int. rel.	Comp. govt.	Pub. law	Polit. theory	Public admin.	Amer. govt.	General politics
Harvard	1	1	3.5	1	2	1	1	2
Yale	2	2	2	5	3	3	2	1
Berkeley	3	3	1	4	4	2	4	3
Chicago	4	4	3.5	3	1	6	3	4
Princeton	5	6	5	2	7	5	7	5
Columbia	6	5	6	7	5	4	6	6
Michigan	7	8	11	6	6	9	8	7
Wisconsin	8.5	10	8	9	8.5	7	5	8
Stanford	8.5	7	10	8	8.5	8	9	9
Cornell	10.5	9	9	10	10.5	10.5	11	11
U.C.L.A.	10.5	11	7	11	10.5	10.5	10	10

$S = 4,536$

$W = .842$

$X^2 = 58.94$

$P \text{ (Ho)} < .001$

related to field commitments (see Chapter 6) is indicated in Table
5. The similarities in perceptions among the several fields are indeed
impressive. With one exception none of the top three departments
over-all is rated less than fourth by the members of any field nor
any of the lowest four departments over-all placed higher than
seventh. The greatest differences between field and over-all rankings
are the four places by which comparative government overrates
U.C.L.A. and downgrades Michigan. Three place differentials occur
when those in American government and politics move Wisconsin
to fifth; public law, Princeton to second; political theory, Chicago
to first; and public law, Yale to fifth. Statistical analysis confirms
what must already be apparent—one may readily dismiss the likelihood that these similarities are chance occurrences.

If all departments, rather than just the prestige group, are
considered, only a handful of differences stands out. To illustrate,
those in international relations and in general politics and processes would raise Northwestern to the top eleven. American politics
would similarly elevate Illinois; those in public administration, Indiana; and public law, Johns Hopkins. Nonetheless, when all these
deviations are taken into account, the evidence is persuasive that
perceptions of departmental excellence are not much influenced by
field commitment.

-5-

The Blessings of Prestige

In the pages immediately preceding, we have described a status or prestige hierarchy which reflects the profession's evaluation of departmental quality. A relatively small group of departments, substantially unchanged in membership over the past four decades, is seen as pre-eminent in the discipline and as superior to the others. We also noted a shifting pattern of doctoral output whereby the more prestigious schools are now producing a minority of our new Ph.D.'s and the less prestigious ones a majority. What are the practical consequences of these two developments?

They are, to put it bluntly, quite disturbing. As Theodore Caplow and Reese McGee have observed of the academic world at large, "Unfortunately, the initial choice of a graduate school sets an indelible mark on the student's career. In many disciplines, men trained at minor universities have virtually no chance of achieving eminence."[1] Only those with degrees from highly regarded schools, they argue, can reasonably hope for appointments at better departments; persons coming from lesser institutions can rarely rise above their doctoral origins. American political science seems to be one of the disciplines subject to these Draconian laws of selection. In our profession, too, the evidence suggests, "where a person gets the doctorate has a determining effect on where he winds up."[2]

According to the 1961 *Directory,* the eleven top departments (the figures are almost identical for both Keniston's group and our own) accounted for 53 per cent of the doctorates then held by American political scientists, although they are *now* producing less than half of our annual output. If we take the latest faculty rosters for the same eleven departments, we find that less than 5 per cent[3] of the political scientists at these schools have doctorates from schools outside the top eleven[4] and that the exceptions occur almost entirely among the institutions in the lower half of the group. One does not have to be a statistician to appreciate what this means. In effect, the possessor of a prestige doctorate has nearly a ten-to-one advantage over someone holding a lesser degree in attaining an appointment at one of the ranking graduate departments.

Nor is the picture any brighter—or, depending on where one stands, dimmer—when we turn to the collegiate level. Berelson speaks of the "forty best colleges." An analysis of the political science appointments at the schools he names (based on a 50 per cent sampling) reveals that almost 80 per cent of the faculty who have doctorates took their degrees at one of the leading eleven departments. Harvard, Chicago, and Columbia together account for more than 40 per cent of the appointees. The pattern is sharpest in the older East Coast institutions, but the same general configuration holds for colleges in other regions as well.

[1] *The Academic Marketplace* (New York: Science Editions, Inc., 1958), p. 225.

[2] Berelson, *op. cit.,* p. 110.

[3] The precise figure would depend upon how one defined faculty. Should we, for example, include professors emeriti, teaching assistants, or visiting professors? The data are so one-sided, though, that it makes really little difference what definition is employed.

[4] We refer here, of course, only to doctorates taken at American universities.

In one sense, though, Berelson did misstate the situation. Where one gets his doctorate does not determine, strictly speaking, where one ends up. Rather, for the great majority of political scientists with doctorates from the lower-rated departments, it determines where they do *not* end up—that is, they obviously do not end up at either the prestigious graduate schools or at the best colleges.

THE RATIONALE OF DISCRIMINATION

These figures, however elementary, leave little doubt that the leading departments pursue a discriminatory policy, insofar as doctoral origins are concerned, in selecting their staff. Now discrimination may refer, albeit this meaning is not currently fashionable, to sophisticated discernment; it may also, and more commonly does, mean unjustified bias. If "good people come only from good departments," as some affirm, this pattern of preferential selection is not indefensible, however unfortunate its consequences for many in the profession. Does the evidence justify the practice?

This is not an easy question to answer. There is no widely accepted standard for objectively measuring the relative abilities of persons trained at prestigious and nonprestigious institutions.[5] There may not even be consensus on what is meant by ability. Furthermore, either a negative or an affirmative answer risks offending half of our colleagues—and an inconclusive answer, all of them. Nevertheless, the issue is of such importance and the comments of many of our respondents revealed such strong convictions on this score that we feel obligated to make at least an exploratory effort.

Great Departments and Great Men

The superior quality of product of the best schools, it is plausible to assume, would be manifested by the superior accomplishments of those trained at these departments. With all due concern

---

[5] Orlans, *op. cit.*, pp. 156–163, reviews some of the criteria most commonly applied.

for the reservations previously listed, we still think the least controversial measure of such accomplishments are the opinions of one's fellow political scientists. We shall, in the next chapter, discuss at some length the profession's ranking of greats—the men generally credited with having made the most significant contributions to the discipline. But we may note here in passing that of the ten men—Beard, Corwin, Dahl, Key, Lasswell, Merriam, Morgenthau, Simon, Truman, and White—named with the greatest frequency by our respondents, one held a foreign degree, Yale and Pennsylvania provided one each, Columbia accounted for two, and all the others came from Chicago.

True, all of the American doctorates were taken at prestige departments.[6] But if this is accepted as proof of the superiority of these departments, should not the heavy concentration of Chicago degrees then be accepted as equally valid evidence that there are substantial qualitative differences between that school and all the others in this group? By this standard, in fact, hardly more than a couple of our most esteemed departments would seem to merit their rating.

Publication as a Measure of Departmental Quality

More than anything else, publication is the standard by which merit is measured in the academic world. And in political science, as we shall see, quantity of publication ranks even higher than quality. Although we do not necessarily endorse this criterion, it enables us to ignore the profound disparity in merit between, say, one article and another and to engage in a simple item count. Following this line of argument, those with doctorates from highly rated departments should manifest a significantly higher publication rate than those with less prestigious degrees.

Readers familiar with Berelson's study will recall that his data, compiled for the purpose of dealing with much the same problem

[6] Pennsylvania was one of the top schools in the 1925 ranking. Purists will, of course, point out that both Corwin and Beard were trained as historians.

for all disciplines, show that this seems to be the case.[7] For a number of reasons, though, we felt that it would be better to tackle the problem anew and decided to analyze the doctoral origins of contributors to the *American Political Science Review* and the *Journal of Politics* for the years 1953, 1957, and 1961. The choice of these three years was arbitrary and intended only to provide an evenly spaced sampling over the past decade. These journals were picked because they are two of the most highly regarded periodicals; because they are general in coverage rather than devoted to a specialized area of political science; and because the number of articles they publish affords a reasonably adequate sample. We counted only articles, excluding reviews, communications to the editor, and the other related items which add so much to the readability of our professional journals.

Our findings can be summarized quite readily. For the three years studied, 80 per cent of the authors in the *Review* and 70 per cent of those in the *Journal of Politics* held prestige doctorates; nonprestige doctorates thus accounted for only 20 and 30 per cent, respectively, of the authorships.[8] Since the profession is now about evenly divided between those holding these two types of doctorates, we seem to have established a prima facie case. Yes—but there may be some doubt as to what has been demonstrated.

Even if we grant that frequency of publication is a fair yardstick by which to measure professional competence—and apparently only a benighted minority denies that this is the standard most often applied (see Chapter 8)—there are still a few offsetting factors which must be taken into consideration. Those with lower-status doctorates are more likely to hold appointments at schools where relatively heavier teaching loads, poorer library facilities, and a paucity of financial resources pose serious obstacles to research and, consequently, to publication. Institutional affiliations, as well as sub-

---

[7] *Op. cit.,* pp. 127, 271–272. For political science, Berelson examined articles published during 1958 in the *American Political Science Review,* the *Political Science Quarterly,* and *World Politics.* The latter two journals, we feel, would hardly include a representative cross section of the discipline among their authors.

[8] Only authors holding an American doctorate were included in our count.

stantive content, may also have some bearing on whether a manuscript is accepted or rejected. If we concede some force to either or both of these arguments, the foregoing percentages can be used to support two quite different lines of reasoning: first, that they prove the superiority of those with good doctorates, who clearly publish the preponderate number of articles, or, second, that they afford impressive evidence of the basic equality of political scientists holding lesser degrees, who still manage to produce a respectable share of our literature despite the grave handicaps under which they labor. There is much to be said, we unequivocally declare, for each of these interpretations.

Doctoral Origins and Attitudes on Professional Issues

A third area in which measurable differences might manifest themselves would be in attitudes toward the major intellectual issues currently facing the profession, although we would emphasize that little is known of the relationship between attitudes and ability and that doctoral training is only one of several factors operative in the process of professional socialization. In any event, such differences did not emerge in our questionnaire responses. Neither in the responses to statements dealing with specific topics nor in the major factors previously mentioned was there any appreciable divergence in the positions taken by the two groups.

THE COSTS OF CASTE

The foregoing evidence is neither conclusive nor unambiguous. Whether there is a real difference in quality between those taking their doctorates at the best and "non-best" departments or whether we have here simply another example of the infinite human capacity for drawing and enforcing essentially irrational distinctions remains for the time being a matter of conjecture, if not controversy. But there is certainly no doubt that persons with a "wrong" degree are largely excluded from appointments at the better schools. As Durkheim observed, "a social fact is to be recognized by the power of external coercion which it exercises over the individual."

The consequences of this practice were perhaps somewhat more tolerable, if no more defensible, in previous decades, when most of the profession took their degrees at this small group of highly prestigious departments. Today this is no longer the case. Over half of our doctorates are being granted by the less well-regarded schools. Instead of discriminating against a minority of the profession, as formerly, we are now in the anomalous position of discriminating against the majority. Other issues aside—and these are not hard to identify even in a profession where many make a virtue of normative neutrality—we must ultimately face up to the following question: Is there such an abundance of creative talent in American political science that we can afford, as a discipline, to treat so substantial a segment of our membership as professional pariahs?

-6-
The Fields of Political Science

The expansion of knowledge which resulted in the emergence of separate disciplines eventually produced a further subdivision of labor into even narrower areas of specialization called, in professional parlance, "fields." As a consequence, the modern scholar normally does not attempt to master his discipline in its entirety. Instead, he limits his attention to one field, or perhaps two, and feels quite satisfied if he can somehow remain generally conversant with developments in other areas. This specialization has been carried further in the natural than in the social sciences, but even in the latter positions are now staffed in terms of a particular field rather than simply by the appointment of an economist, a sociologist, or a political scientist.

At any time, the component fields of a discipline provide a convenient way of describing its boundaries and of identifying the subject matter regarded as falling within its purview. To some degree, however, the fields—and hence the boundaries—are always in a state of flux. Some fields expand, others contract. New fields emerge, older ones decline and disappear. The new field may evidence a real shift of substantive interest or little more than the acceptance of some currently fashionable terminology. Important discoveries and advances may be made in some fields while others remain quiescent. Members of a profession will find certain areas more—and others, less—attractive, and the distribution of specialists will change accordingly. Ideas and techniques developed in one field may be enthusiastically adopted or vigorously opposed in others; contrariwise, intellectual issues may cut across, as well as between, fields.

Sooner or later, of course, specialization becomes a mixed blessing for any discipline. It has undoubtedly consequences of vast benefit. Specialization makes possible the development of the expertise and the intensive concentration of energies necessary for successful assaults on otherwise insurmountable problems. It is unlikely that the gains achieved by scientists in recent decades could have been made without this division of labor; it is equally unlikely that the modern discipline could function without such compartmentalization.

But specialization also exacts a heavy tariff. The perennial difficulties of communicating across subject matter boundaries may arise within the discipline itself. The number and the definition of fields in a discipline may become a matter of bitter controversy. The diversity of interests and values which specialization brings can readily constitute a threat to the stability of the parent science. In some instances, in fact, the fields of a discipline seem to be quasi-independent entities precariously held together by a common tradition and history, but with little assurance that centripetal rather than centrifugal tendencies will ultimately prevail.

These considerations, then, provide the background for this chapter—one devoted to the fields of American political science. We shall attempt to answer such questions as these: What are the major fields of political science today? What is the distribution of the profession among these several fields? How do political scientists rate the importance of the work being done in each of these fields? To what degree does field commitment affect one's stand on behavioralism and the adequacy of the discipline? Which fields tend to be most separatist? Which least? And, perhaps the most crucial of all: In what direction are the several fields in American political science tending, toward cohesion or toward separatism?

FIELD DISTRIBUTION IN AMERICAN POLITICAL SCIENCE

Each of the three post–World War II editions (1948, 1953, and 1961) of the *Directory* of the American Political Science Association provides two sources of information about field affiliations—first, the member's own biographical entry; second, an appended roster of the membership classified by field of specialization, based on that entry. Although useful for other purposes, from our viewpoint these rosters had several limiting characteristics. They were derived, in effect, from a forced-choice method of field identification whereby the respondent checked off his fields of specialization from a prepared list. This approach provides data in readily manageable form, but, since the analytical categories are already decided, it tends to predetermine the results obtained. Furthermore, the biographical form used in gathering material for the 1948 edition permitted as many as five field identifications without clear indication of priority; those for the 1953 and 1961 editions, three; and the aforementioned field rosters gave equal weight to each of these multiple choices. Whatever its merits, this procedure fails to provide reliable information about the respondent's *primary* field of specialization. Finally, the shifting nature of the three lists (1948, 1953, 1961) on which the member was asked to indicate his fields creates problems if one attempts a comparison of the three sets of responses.

Despite the foregoing limitations, the data in the three directories are not without value if they are treated as suggestive rather than conclusive. To get a more consistent basis of comparison than that afforded by the rosters, we took a systematic 20 per cent sample of all (nonstudent) members listed in the two later directories and developed the following field analysis from this sample:

TABLE 6

FIELD DISTRIBUTION BASED ON DIRECTORY SAMPLES

Field	Per cent* 1961 Directory	Per cent* 1953 Directory
International relations	36.9	31.8
Comparative government	34.9	29.9
Public law	16.4	18.1
Public administration	26.4	34.9
Political theory	29.7	17.5
American government and politics†	58.1	49.5

* Total exceeds 100 per cent since respondents could identify as many as three fields.

† This is essentially a catchall classification since the analytic categories used in the directories did not permit a meaningful comparison of responses covering general politics, American politics, parties, and public opinion as fields.

There seems to have been a substantial growth of interest only in political theory. International relations, comparative government, and American government and politics showed a modest gain; public law held essentially constant; and there was a sharp drop in public administration. To repeat, however: These data are drawn from biographical entries in which three fields of specialization are stated, and there is considerable doubt that they afford a reliable picture of field distribution for either year, let alone of trends between 1953 and 1961.

Field Distribution, 1963 Study

In structuring the field-distribution aspect of our inquiry, we deliberately sought to limit respondents to one field and to have them describe the field in their own words. Accordingly, we asked that they answer, as they saw fit, the query: "If you had to identify yourself with a SINGLE field in political science, which one would it be?" The reason for restricting their choice has already been given. The free-response device minimized the degree to which our own conceptions would predetermine the answers given.

The four hundred some replies were coded, grouped, and then organized into the sevenfold classification employed in this study—international relations, American government and politics, comparative government, political theory, public administration, general politics and political processes, and public law. International law was subsumed under international relations and constitutes about 15 per cent of this field. Those giving an area-studies specialization were classified under comparative government, making up just slightly more than 5 per cent of that group. The three or four methodologists wound up in political theory. All specific commitments to state and local government were assigned to American government and politics. These dispensations, we would say, are as reasonable as any others that might have been made.

Four per cent of the respondents failed to indicate their field. Approximately the same number of replies could not be satisfactorily fitted into any of our categories and were simply designated as "miscellaneous." Some examples of these are, "legislation and administration of modern technology," "adaptation and modifications in political institutions as a result of social change," and "politico-economic-legal theory." The field pattern which emerged from the data is shown in Table 7. This distribution, to repeat, is in terms of the *single* field with which the respondents felt most closely associated.

International relations is the most popular field, with American

TABLE 7

FIELD DISTRIBUTION OF AMERICAN POLITICAL SCIENTISTS, 1963

Field	Number in sample	Per cent of total
International relations	87	20.2
American government and politics	74	17.2
Comparative government	53	12.3
Political theory	53	12.3
Public administration	50	11.6
General politics and political processes	43	10.0
Public law	39	9.1
Not classifiable	15	3.5
Not indicated	17	3.9
Total	431	100.1

government and politics a fairly close second. The remaining fields are approximately equal in size, with less than four percentage points separating the third- and the seventh-ranking areas. The differences in the nature of the data, to repeat, make it hazardous to compare the results in this table with those in Table 6.

EVALUATION OF FIELDS

What accounts for the popularity of one field and the relative unpopularity of another? The various explanations range from a theory of psychological types to practical considerations of employment opportunities.[1] One of the more plausible suppositions is that there is a relationship between the prevailing assessment of the work being done in the several fields and the tendency of those in the

[1] Ann Roe, *The Psychology of Occupations* (New York: John Wiley & Sons, Inc., 1956). For another approach, see Raymond A. Katzell, "Personal Values, Job Satisfaction, and Job Behavior," in Henry Borow, ed., *Man in a World at Work* (Boston: Houghton Mifflin Co., 1964).

profession to specialize in one area or another. Actually, three distinct problems are involved here: (1) How do American political scientists rate the seven fields in terms of accomplishment? (2) Is there any correlation between this rating and field popularity? and (3) How does field commitment affect one's evaluation of his own field and of other fields? The first and third queries are probably of greater import than the second.

Fields: Most and Least Significant Work

In seeking answers to these questions, we asked our respondents to identify, again in their own words, the field(s) of political science in which they felt that the *most* and the *least* significant work was being done (Items B-3 and B-4 of questionnaire).[2] Few people made more than one entry under either heading, although room was provided for several. The replies were then classified according to our sevenfold system and the ratio of favorable (that is, most significant) to unfavorable (that is, least significant) mentions computed for each field. The standing of the fields was based on this ratio. A ratio of 1.00 indicates that a field was mentioned an equal number of times under each heading; of more than 1.00, that favorable mentions outnumbered the unfavorable. Table 8 gives the rank order and ratio score for each field.

In the esteem of the profession, comparative government and general politics almost tie for first place. International relations, public administration, and American government and politics constitute, in that order, a middle group. The bottom of the ranking almost replicates the top, with public law and political theory running neck and neck—if this is the appropriate figure of speech—for last place.

A comparison of the actual scores earned by the several fields is even more revealing. The ratio of favorable to unfavorable mentions

---

[2] We do not know, of course, just what factors enter into the feeling that the work being done in a particular field is or is not very significant. For some people, this determination might flow from familiarity with the work of one or two especially able—or incompetent—people working in the field; for others, it might reflect a much broader basis of judgment.

TABLE 8

FIELDS RANKED BY SIGNIFICANCE OF CURRENT WORK:
RATIO OF MOST SIGNIFICANT TO LEAST SIGNIFICANT MENTIONS

Order	Field	Ratio
1	Comparative government	3.78
2	General politics and political processes	3.76
3	International relations	1.43
4	Public administration	1.02
5	American government and politics	.721
6	Public law	.394
7	Political theory	.367

for the two top fields runs about 300 per cent higher than for the middle group and almost 1,000 per cent greater than for public law and political theory. In the middle group itself there is almost a 100 per cent difference in score between the third- and the fifth-ranking fields. In fact, American government and politics may more properly belong with the two lowest fields, since all three received scores of less than 1.00.

This is, perhaps, the critical point. The actual location of a field on this hierarchy may have less bearing on the long-run viability of a given field than whether the accomplishments of those working in the area are seen as falling, on balance, closer to the more significant than to the least significant end of the scale. A predominance of the latter type of rating, as in the cases of public law and political theory, suggests an unhealthy situation both for the fields and for the discipline.

In working up the ratios in Table 8, it became clear that two fields, international relations and American government and politics, were being adversely affected by unfavorable evaluations of one of their component subareas—international law in the case of the former, state and local government in the latter. If the ratios in Table 8 are recalculated to exclude all references, favorable or unfavorable, to international law and to state and local government, the rank order changes only slightly. American government and politics moves to fourth position, and public administration drops to fifth while the position of international relations remains the same. But the differences in the magnitudes of the ratios is very substantial. International relations, without the burden of international law, climbs from 1.43 to 2.20; American government and politics, without state and local government, soars from .721 to a very respectable 1.77.

Nevertheless, neither international law nor state and local government, we would argue, can properly be regarded as fields in themselves, and, as subareas, they most appropriately fit in the larger fields to which we have assigned them. Still, the pattern of responses was so consistent and so hostile that the phenomenon merits explicit recognition.

Field Rating and Popularity

The relationship between the popularity of a field and the reputation it enjoys in the profession can be readily handled by comparing the rank orders in Table 8 with those in Table 7. The importance of the work being done in a field apparently has little to do with its popularity as an area of specialization within the discipline.

Field Commitment as a Variable in Ranking Fields

The question here is how much field affiliation influences perceptions of the work being done in the other areas of the discipline. We normally could anticipate the operation of a halo effect, and, given the disparity in the populations comprising the fields, this could have considerable impact on rank order and scores alike. Table 9 presents the data developed to determine the degree to which such a bias is reflected in the ratings.

TABLE 9

RANK ORDER RATINGS OF ALL FIELDS BY MEMBERS IDENTIFIED WITH EACH*

Rater's field	Rank order ratings						
	Int. rel.	Comp. govt.	Pub. law	Polit. theory	Pub. admin.	Amer. govt.	Gen. pol.
International relations	3	2	6	7	5	4	1
Comparative government	5	1	7	6	4	3	2
Public law	7	5.5	2	4	3	5.5	1
Political theory	2	1	3	4	6	7	5
Public administration	4.5	3	6	7	2	4.5	1
American government and politics	5	2	7	6	3	4	1
General politics and political processes	3	1	6	7	5	4	2
Over-all	3	1	6	7	4	5	2

S = 649.25

Coefficient of concordance (W) = .473

P (Ho) < .01

* Ratings are based on ratio of "most significant" to "least significant" responses on field contributions questions.

We will operationally define halo effect as rating one's own field *more* than one place higher than the position assigned to it by the profession as a whole. People in public law, political theory, and public administration seem especially susceptible to this frailty, whereas American government and politics and international relations specialists see themselves much as do the others. The measure utilized obviously makes it impossible for those in general politics and in comparative government to overrate themselves. Contrariwise, it would have been possible for all fields other than public law and political theory to show a reverse halo effect, that is, to underrate themselves. It is heartening to note that not a single field succumbed to this temptation.

In addition to dealing with the halo effect, Table 9 tells something else of considerable interest. It shows the different rankings given to each field by political scientists specializing in each of the seven areas. Five of the seven fields rated comparative government either first or second; six of seven did the same for general politics. At the other end of the scale, five of seven fields placed public law and political theory either sixth or seventh. In almost every case, the dissenters were in theory and law. The field with the widest range of assessments was international relations, which earned ratings running from second to seventh place.

When the entire array of rankings is analyzed statistically, it becomes clear that persons in the several fields use fundamentally similar standards in evaluating the work being done in each of these areas.

FIELD COMMITMENT AND INTELLECTUAL ISSUES

The foregoing finding is a significant indication of consensus on a matter in which separatism might have been expected. Does it follow that the association between field commitment and attitudes on intellectual issues is also slight? Analysis of variance discloses that the differences between fields on the behavioral factor are so great that it would be extremely hazardous to consider them fortuitous.[3] The most behaviorally oriented of all fields is general politics and processes, with public administration in second place. At the other end of the continuum are political theory, far and away the most hostile to the behavioral persuasion, and public law.

Disagreement over the adequacy of the discipline is not nearly so sharp. Of all the fields, American government and international relations find the discipline most adequate; comparative government and theory find it most wanting. But the variance between fields is insufficient to warrant the conclusion that these differences are not happenstance.

However valuable in identifying the topics on which separatism exists, analysis of variance is not well suited for isolating the field(s) most out of step with the majority of the profession. Nor, for that matter, is any other statistic with which we are familiar. The best method we could devise for measuring separatism on the intellectual issues is admittedly a crude one, yet it does provide a rough way of ranking fields by the extent to which they deviate from the discipline as a whole. For each of the twenty-six issue statements, the responses in each field were compared with those for all other fields. For example, we compared the responses of all those in American government and politics with those of the remaining six fields and determined the number of questions on which the differences between the two sets of replies reached a set level ($P < .05$) of statistical significance.[4] There are four such questions. Each of the other fields was analyzed in similar fashion. By this measure political theory is far and away the field most out of step. Political theorists hold views that differ sharply from those of their colleagues on ten of the twenty-six issues. The field with the next largest number of widely divergent views, public administration, differs on only five questions. General politics, as American government, showed separatism on four items, whereas international relations, comparative government, and public law deviated on only one apiece.

We would not want to place undue reliance on a metric so lacking in elegance. Nevertheless it does support the conclusion that,

---

[3] Nathan Jaspen's 7094 program for the one-way analysis of variance was used for this computation.

[4] T tests were used for this purpose.

except for political theory, differences in outlook tend to be rather well distributed in the fields. There is a good deal of consensus among all fields but theory on intellectual issues other than behavioralism. Comforting though this high degree of consensus may be to the members of the discipline, they surely cannot avoid being troubled by the extent to which the political theorists hold separatist views. For if it is true, as is so often contended, that theory is the core of any discipline and that no discipline can rise much above its theorists, political science has cause for concern. To be sure, the function of serving as theorists for the discipline may have been assumed by those who, for one reason or another, designate themselves by some other name. If so, this is an explanation which raises far more problems than it resolves.

COHESION AND SEPARATISM: A BALANCE SHEET

The nature of our inquiry imposes the unhappy obligation to conclude this chapter with an evaluation of the relative strength of these two forces. Do field attachments threaten the integrity of political science as a discipline?

There can be no question that field commitment has a definite relationship to attitudes toward professional issues. As we have seen, it is associated with differences in assessing the importance of work done in the various areas of political science, in the position taken on behavioralism, and in the views expressed on the specific issues treated by our twenty-six propositions. Furthermore, as we shall see in subsequent chapters, it is also associated with markedly divergent judgments of journal prestige and of the significance of the contributions to the discipline made by specific political scientists. In all of these respects, field commitments seem to produce substantial conflicts of opinion. Field of specialization, together with the factors of behavioralism and adequacy of the profession, is certainly one of the three most important variables which affect values and perceptions in the discipline on the problems examined in this study.

On the other side of the ledger, the differences in attitudes and values among the seven fields, although not insubstantial, are by no means great. The areas of agreement are much wider than those of conflict, nor do the disagreements reach a magnitude which suggests massive and disruptive controversy within the profession. On balance, we would therefore conclude that the profession enjoys fundamental consensus cutting across most, if not all, of its major fields and that these divergences in opinion do not, as matters now stand, seriously threaten the integrity and cohesion of the discipline.

This judgment is subject to two qualifications. We do not know just what the trend has been in political science. We would obviously be better able to assess the present situation if we knew the direction in which the profession has moved during the past decade or two. Are the several fields coming closer together or moving farther apart in outlook? Second, we have no standard by which to compare the situation in political science with that in other disciplines. How much conflict and controversy can a discipline survive? What is the critical point of discord beyond which fission occurs? These are questions which we cannot yet answer. They call, as we point out in Appendix C, for a study much broader than the one undertaken here.

-7-

Political Science's Hall of Fame

The most appropriate text for this chapter would have been the biblical injunction, "By their fruits shall ye know them." This precept certainly suggests the major reasons for concerning ourselves with the persons recognized as great men by the profession. Such recognition serves, of course, to identify those who are seen as having made the most substantial contributions to the discipline. It tells us, in addition, a good deal about the discipline itself—the existence or absence of consensus, the type of accomplishment which commends itself to one's colleagues, and the level of attainment which marks an individual as outstanding in American political science.

When political scientists, relaxing from the burdens of teaching, research, molding public opinion, and shaping governmental policy, gather together in convivial discourse, this subject is almost sure to come up. Sooner or later the conversation will come around to the work that X is doing, how it compares with that of Y and Z, and, ultimately, how all three measure up against those who are already enshrined as true masters—if the discussants can agree on the last point.

The psychological mechanisms operative here are probably the same in all learned disciplines. To the degree that political scientists have strong convictions, they discern merit, if not greatness, in those who are the leading proponents of the theories to which they are personally committed. This identification reinforces, in turn, belief in the merit of those ideas. The dual process of identification and evaluation provides, moreover, a standard whereby political scientists can assure themselves that what they have done, are doing, or plan to do is also of a creditable order of significance.

Third, discussions of individual eminence, despite the heat and fury they occasionally evoke, serve both as a sign of professional kinship and as a means of cementing these bonds. Political scientists may quarrel over which persons are truly pre-eminent, but the dispute itself testifies to the belief, essential to any discipline, that serious contributions to human knowledge are being made by its membership. Though political scientists do not command, individually or collectively, the public recognition enjoyed by more fortunate professions through such prestigious devices as the Nobel prizes, political scientists can at least assure themselves—and, hopefully, practitioners of the other social sciences as well—that the great men in political science have made discoveries which, in the framework of their enterprise, are no less meritorious.

In any discipline, greatness is to some degree a matter of opinion. In political science, far more so than in the hard sciences, greatness tends to be a function of agreement, given the absence of accepted or objective standards. This chapter deals, therefore, not with greatness in any intrinsic sense, but with a surrogate for it— the opinions of the profession. These opinions may reflect a mature evaluation or only a transient mood, but, whatever injustices are entailed, they represent the most defensible criterion presently available—the verdict of one's peers. In this judgment, two distinct elements are involved: first, the actual identification of major figures; second, the reasoning on which the selections are based. The latter is a highly complex problem which can be adequately explored only by detailed interview. The former, however, can be readily ascertained via questionnaire.

Toward this end, Item C-1 of the questionnaire asked, "In your judgment, which political scientists have made the *most* significant contributions to the discipline?" Using the responses to this item, we shall seek to answer a number of questions. Among these will be: Who are the persons whose accomplishments are seen as most significant? To what extent is there some consensus on this score? What variables are related to these judgments? What type of achievements seem most readily to gain recognition? And, underlying all of these queries, what do these evaluations tell us about the discipline itself?

THE IMMORTALS

American political science, as a formally organized discipline, is now about sixty years old. Since not all respondents might be equally familiar with both the earlier and later history of the profession, we felt that it would be desirable to have them distinguish, in their nominations for political science's hall of fame, between those who made the most significant contributions prior to 1945 and from 1945 to the present. Each respondent was free to enter as many names as he wished under either heading. Most made one or two nominations for each era; few named more than three; about a fifth failed to make any entry at all. The number of times a person was mentioned was tallied and then divided by the entire number of respondents (431). The resulting percentage constitutes, we believe, a useful index of recognition.

The rankings produced by our inquiry are shown in Table 10. All those who received ten or more nominations in either period are included. Four men—Lasswell, White, Friedrich, and Schattschneider—therefore appear on both listings.

TABLE 10[1]

RANKING OF GREAT MEN

	Pre-1945				Post-1945		
Rank	Name	N	Named by per cent of respondents	Rank	Name	N	Named by per cent of respondents
1	Charles E. Merriam	131	37.4	1	V. O. Key, Jr.	128	36.6
2	Harold D. Lasswell	106	30.3	2	David B. Truman	70	20.0
3	Leonard D. White	57	16.3	3	Hans J. Morgenthau	69	19.7
4	Charles A. Beard	56	16.0	4	Robert A. Dahl	68	19.4
5	Edward S. Corwin	52	14.9	5	Harold D. Lasswell	56	16.0
6	Arthur F. Bentley	37	10.6	6	Herbert A. Simon	50	14.3
7	Woodrow Wilson	34	9.7	7.5	Gabriel A. Almond	31	8.9
8	Pendleton Herring	23	6.6	7.5	David Easton	31	8.9
9	Quincy Wright	18	5.1	9	Leo Strauss	20	5.7
10	Frederic A. Ogg	17	4.9	10	Carl J. Friedrich	18	5.1
11	Frank J. Goodnow	15	4.3	11	Charles S. Hyneman	15	4.3
12.5	Harold J. Laski	14	4.0	12	E. E. Schattschneider	14	4.0
12.5	Arthur N. Holcombe	14	4.0	13.5	Peter H. Odegard	13	3.7
14.5	Francis W. Coker	12	3.4	13.5	Richard C. Snyder	13	3.7
14.5	Carl J. Friedrich	12	3.4	15	Leonard D. White	11	3.1
16	George H. Sabine	11	3.1	17	James M. Burns	10	2.9
17.5	Harold F. Gosnell	10	2.9	17	Karl W. Deutsch	10	2.9
17.5	E. E. Schattschneider	10	2.9	17	Heinz Eulau	10	2.9
				17	Dwight Waldo	10	2.9

[1] We have previously argued that the ultimate goal of most political scientists is an appointment at one of the prestigious graduate schools. The careers of the eminent scholars listed above certainly support this contention. Almost any one of them, it is reasonable to assume, enjoyed considerable latitude of choice as to the type of institution at which he would serve. Almost, but not quite, every one of them elected to go to—or stay at—a ranking department.

The same data could, of course, be used to support a different, though not contradictory proposition: that it is much easier to attain eminence if one holds an appointment at a prestigious school. At present we do not see any practical way of coming to grips with this problem.

As we are simply reporting opinions about greatness, no useful purpose would be served by commenting favorably or unfavorably on the presence or absence of specific names. We would like, however, to call attention to one of the most striking characteristics of this tabulation—the apparent lack of consensus as to the men who have made significant contributions to political science. A marked divergence of outlook is evident even when we look at the three figures who stand highest in the estimation of the profession— Lasswell, Merriam, and Key.

Lasswell, high on the list for both periods and far and away the one individual most often named, is still the choice of less than half the respondents. For Merriam and Key the level of recognition is barely one in three; when we get to third place on either ranking it drops below one in five; and at tenth position, by normal standards still an honorific position, barely one in twenty concur. This diffusion of opinion poses a problem to which we shall return.

THE ELEMENTS OF EMINENCE

Even a casual examination of the names making up the two rosters suggests that several very different standards were operative in designating those who made the most significant contributions. Perhaps this can more readily be seen for the pre-1945 group, for which we have a better historical perspective, than for the later ranking.

In the sciences, the distinction of having made a major contribution is reserved for those whose intellectual originality results in new analytic tools or concepts and eventually in the charting of previously unexplored domains. The highest plaudits are traditionally reserved for these rare "idea" men.[2] Of those on the pre-1945 honor roll, Harold D. Lasswell most clearly represents this type.

[2] "Academic institutions and genius," observed Charles Horton Cooley, "are in the nature of things antithetical. Professors," he continued, "like successful lawyers or doctors, are just hard-working men of some talent." Cited by David Riesman, *Life and the Student: Roadside Notes on Human Nature, Society and Letters* (New York: Alfred A. Knopf, Inc., 1951), p. 9.

Some might argue that Bentley, too, was an innovator. Perhaps, but Lasswell stands on his own accomplishments, whereas Bentley's fame is retrospective and largely owing to the subsequent development and application of his ideas by David B. Truman.[3] If there is a second political scientist—and here there might be a jurisdictional dispute with the historians—who fits comfortably into this category, we would be inclined to nominate Charles A. Beard.

At another level, there is the individual whose contribution has been that of systematizing a new field in the discipline and, in the process, of molding it in the image of his own thought. Woodrow Wilson may be credited with having initially called the attention of American political scientists to the need for a systematic study of public administration and Frank J. Goodnow with having been among the first to make the attempt. Yet it was Leonard D. White who was primarily instrumental in structuring the field during the formative decades of its development and of guiding it in the direction of his own approach and ideas. It is not irrelevant to add that Herbert A. Simon, who has played much the same role in public administration during the post-1945 period, received his training under White.

This suggests the third type of contribution political scientists honor—that of the man who functions as a catalyst, who has the ability to detect and attract promise, to encourage experimentation, and who serves as a symbol and a rallying point for new intellectual movements in the discipline. Whatever Charles E. Merriam's scholarly attainments—and these were by no means inconsequential—in the final assessment his contribution is to be found not so much in his own writings as in the accomplishments of those who became part of, or were trained at, Merriam's department. The "Chicago school," which dominated political science for almost two decades and whose influence is still felt today, was his real legacy.

A fourth criterion suggested by the ranking is that of having written a textbook which has successfully weathered the onslaughts

---

[3] For a somewhat more laudatory view of Bentley's contribution, see Norman Jacobson, "Causality and Time in Political Process," *American Political Science Review*, LVIII, No. 1 (1964), 15–22.

of time and competition. For almost two decades, this was the distinction of White's *Introduction to the Study of Public Administration;* in similar fashion, Ogg and Ray's fact-laden tome held steadfast against the assaults of rival volumes and students. But the most solid claim for an outstanding text is incontrovertibly that of George H. Sabine, whose magisterial *History of Political Theory* remains the envy and the despair of succeeding generations of political theorists. The folklore of the discipline may eulogize the virtues and rewards of original research, but the author of a successful textbook is not without a fair measure of honor (see Chapter 8).

Last, there is what we might call the "organizational" standard—a significant contribution in services to the profession in its organized, institutional capacity. Perhaps more than anything else, this accounts for Ogg's place among the leading figures of the profession. For "nigh onto twenty years," the contents of the *American Political Science Review* reflected Ogg's understanding of the subject matter with which political science and political scientists should properly be concerned. Many will challenge the wisdom of his ideas, but few will deny his devotion to his task. In paradoxical fashion, Ogg played, at one end of the professional spectrum, a part not too dissimilar from that of Merriam at the other, opposed though the two men were in outlook and objectives.

The foregoing typology is obviously our own construct, since we have no firsthand knowledge of the standards actually applied by the respondents in making their choices. We do not claim that these five categories exhaust all the possibilities, that they neatly account for everyone listed, or even that a fair case could not be made for assigning people to a category other than that suggested. Granting all of this, we still maintain that the rankings reflect diverse conceptions of what is a most significant contribution and that our fivefold scheme affords a plausible theory of the various criteria operative in the pre-1945 nominations.

How well does it fit the roster of more recent greats? Fairly well, we would say, although it may be too soon to tell. But—and we wish to stress this point—the types of achievement which gain a man eminence in a discipline may change from one period to another. As a discipline matures, it develops new imperatives and new standards as well as new ideas. At one stage, innovation may be in order; at another, it is the synthesizer, the harmonizer, and the eclectic who are seen as making the key contributions. This is a subject which calls far more for systematic study than for exegetical ingenuity.

VARIABLES OPERATIVE IN PERCEPTION OF GREATNESS

The type of ranking we have presented is inevitably a product both of the attributes of those who are assessed and of those who make the assessment. We have dealt briefly with the former in the preceding pages; here our focus shifts from the characteristics of the greats to those of the persons making the nominations.

Perceptions of greatness vary with the interests and values of the rater. We would therefore expect that differences in the intellectual commitments of our respondents would be in some measure reflected by differences in their recognition of most significant contributions. Is this expectation supported when we introduce the three major variables—behavioralism, adequacy of the profession, and field of specialization? For the purposes of this analysis, we will combine the votes received by each person for each of the two periods and then take the top ten individuals. The resulting rank order therefore differs slightly from either of those in Table 10 .

Behavioralism and Adequacy of the Profession

Behavioralism, we need hardly repeat, is the leading issue currently facing the profession. Although most political scientists do not seem to have violent feelings on the matter, two relatively small groups do take strong positions, pro and con. Table 11 shows the manner in which commitment on this issue is related to perceptions of greatness.

All in all, the relationship is not very strong. True, those who are staunchly probehavioral tend to see greater merit in the work

TABLE 11

RANKING OF TEN GREATS BY RESPONDENTS HAVING EXTREME
SCORES ON BEHAVIORALISM AND ADEQUACY FACTORS*

| | Behavioralism | | Adequacy | | Over-all |
Greats	Pro	Anti	More	Less	rank
Lasswell	1	7	3	1	1
Merriam	3	1	1	3	2
Key	2	2	2	2	3
Morgenthau†	8	4.5	5	8	4
Truman	5	8.5	9	7	5
White‡	7	4.5	4	6	6.5
Dahl	4	10	7.5	5	6.5
Corwin§	10	3	6	9	8.5
Beard	9	6	7.5	10	8.5
Simon	6	8.5	10	4	10

* Higher than plus one standard deviation and lower than minus one
standard deviation.
† Includes six pre-1945 votes.
‡ Includes eleven post-1945 votes.
§ Includes four post-1945 votes.

$Tau = .45$	$Tau = .07$
$Z = 1.68$	$Z < .362$
$P (Ho) > .05$	$P (Ho) > .05$

of Lasswell, Dahl, and Simon and less in that of Corwin, Morgenthau, and Beard than do members of the opposing school. But the
divergence is by no means so great as someone familiar with the
rancor of the debate between the two factions might have predicted.
It does not reach statistical significance.[4]

The data in Table 11 also show that assessments of the greats
are even less a function of the adequacy of the discipline factor than
they are of the behavioralism factor. Those who regard the discipline as adequate tend to favor Merriam over Lasswell and to favor

[4] Kendall's rank correlation coefficient was the test used here.

Corwin and Morgenthau over Truman and Dahl. In only one instance, though, do the groups differing most severely on this factor place any great more than three ranks apart.

Field of Specialization as a Variable in Recognition

Another picture emerges, however, when we turn to the next variable, field of specialization. More than any other, this seems to be the dominant element in shaping assessments of individual contributions to political science. Table 12, which shows the manner in which the ten most eminent figures are ranked by respondents when the latter are classified by field affiliation, vividly illustrates the impact of this bias. These differences cannot be regarded as happenstance.[5]

There is most agreement on Lasswell and Merriam. Six of the seven fields gave a first or second place to the former and a second or third place to the latter. Other than Lasswell, only Key and Morgenthau received a first-place rating. In addition, everyone except Lasswell, Merriam, and Key was ranked ninth or tenth by the members of at least one field.

The distance between the highest and lowest rankings achieved by our ten leading figures on Table 12 averages in excess of six places, more than half the possible range. Not even the three giants are immune—Lasswell moves between first place to a tie for fourth; Key from first to seventh; and Merriam from second to seventh position. The sharpest disagreement is over Morgenthau, who, fourth on the over-all ranking, ranges from a tie for first to tenth place. White and Corwin, who move between third and tenth, are the next most volatile.

The role played by field affiliation casts considerable light on why the profession finds it so hard to agree upon its great figures, a phenomenon mentioned earlier. Nevertheless, field still falls short of being a complete explanation for the apparent lack of consensus. Lasswell, for example, received support from at least 30 per cent

---

[5] Both the Kendall coefficient of concordance and the Kruskal-Wallis one-way analysis of variance show $P(Ho) < .001$.

TABLE 12

RANKING OF TEN GREATS BY FIELD OF RESPONDENTS

	Int. rel.	Comp. govt.	Pub. law	Polit. theory	Pub. admin.	Amer. govt.	Gen. pol.	Over-all rank
Lasswell	1.5	1	1	1	4.5	2	1	1
Merriam	3	2	7	2	2	3	3	2
Key	7	4	2.5	3	1	1	2	3
Morgenthau*	1.5	3	10	7.5	10	9.5	9	4
Truman	6	6	5	9	8	5.5	5	5
White†	4.5	10	8	7.5	3	4	6	6.5
Dahl	9.5	5	4	6	6.5	5.5	4	6.5
Corwin‡	9.5	7	2.5	4.5	6.5	7	10	8.5
Beard	4.5	9	6	4.5	9	8	7	8.5
Simon	8	8	9	10	4.5	9.5	8	10

* Includes six pre-1945 votes.
† Includes eleven post-1945 votes.
‡ Includes four post-1945 votes.

W = 504
X^2 = 31.75
P (Ho) < .001
Df = 9

of the persons in six of the seven fields, but the support of more than 50 per cent from only general politics (with 65 per cent.) Key was listed by 56 per cent of those in this field and 50 per cent of those in American government and politics. No other luminary received as much as 50 per cent of the votes from any field. Moreover, although several men got almost no support from one field or another (international relations gave two votes each to Dahl and Corwin; comparative government, one to White and two to Beard; and public law, one to Morgenthau), only two greats, White and Morgenthau, received as many as half of their nominations from as few as two fields.

Age as a Variable in the Identification of Greats

Age has been introduced as a variable in this study only in those few instances where it might reasonably have a direct bearing on the subject under consideration. The identification of outstanding political scientists seemed to be such a place, since the normal tendency is for persons to choose their idols after their own image. Although the profession is now predominantly "youngish middle-aged," a description which charitably allows some latitude of interpretation, it was only natural to assume that the younger members would incline to the selection of younger heroes and that the more mature members would be likely to vote for those whose deeds have stood the test of time.

This theory had only one defect—it was not supported by the data. When we examined the voting patterns according to a five-fold classification of respondents' age, it was evident that age accounts for very little of the disagreement observed. There were some differences between the older and the younger political scientists, with the latter inclined to think more highly of Truman and Dahl and less well of Corwin and White than do their elders. Notwithstanding these slight disparities of response, the five groups tended to be far more like than unlike in their perceptions of the profession's great men.

SOME UNRESOLVED QUESTIONS

In describing the rankings of great political scientists, in examining the characteristics of those named, and in analyzing the manner in which the several variables seemed to relate to perceptions of greatness, we have touched on three points which warrant brief comment.

The rankings presented in Table 10 reflect the views of the profession as of mid-1963. Do they represent well-crystallized and stable opinions, or are they more realistically to be understood as essentially casual and transient judgments? Both elements are undoubtedly present, but in what proportion? This is clearly a matter of some moment: To what extent are perceptions of significant work influenced by short-lived intellectual fads? To what extent do they hold constant? The answers can come only from similar inquiries in the years ahead.

Next, there is the question of the evaluative criteria employed by the profession. We have suggested what some of these might be. If it is valuable—and we think it is—to know which men are seen as making the most significant contributions, it is no less valuable to ascertain the standards that are being applied in making this determination. In fact, we can think of few areas of investigation which would be as instructive in casting light on the manner in which the discipline functions. Exploration of this subject would require, however, techniques far more sensitive and discriminating than are possible in a questionnaire approach.

Finally, there is the curious lack of consensus in recognizing great contributors to political science. The several variables, as we have seen, fail to provide an adequate explanation for the diffusion of opinion observed. Although we would doubt that the same scattering of responses would occur in the physical sciences, it may be that a broader continuum of opinion on this subject is not entirely unique in the social sciences. Lacking comparable data for other disciplines, one can only speculate.

There is another possibility which we are obliged to mention—
that the low index of recognition springs less from divergent standards of judgment than from a pervasive conviction that there are
few men in the profession who have made truly significant contributions. To the measure that this explanation is valid, we would
have cause to be concerned with the well-being of American political science, for it is essential to a learned discipline that its practitioners believe that what they are doing is worth doing and that
they are doing it reasonably well.

-8-

The Road to Success—
Who Gets What How

As academicians and scholars, American political scientists are dedicated, above all, to the discovery and transmission of knowledge. But as human beings, consumers, husbands, and fathers (and, occasionally, wives and mothers), they cannot be totally uninterested in the material and psychological rewards attendant on professional advancement or completely unconcerned with the advance of their personal careers. How do they assess the relative importance of the several attributes generally seen as having a bearing on success in the discipline?

An unambiguous operational definition of success was obviously necessary if the inquiry was to be manageable and the findings meaningful. As our pretest panelists pointed out, several roads to success are open to academic man and movement along these, to push the metaphor a last step, is not always subject to the same traffic regulations. After considering a number of alternatives, we decided that success could be most productively equated with "the ability to get offers from other schools." The respondents raised no objections to this definition, although some noted—and we completely agree—that success can also be defined in radically different terms.

Pretest comment also proved helpful in identifying the various elements or attributes believed to be related to success. The original listing contained only six items; the revised version was expanded to ten. Respondents were asked to rate each of these on a four-point scale—"a great deal," "some," "very little," and "none" (C-6, questionnaire). Additional space was provided for other attributes to be written in, if deemed relevant, but the ten-item listing seemed to be reasonably exhaustive.[1] The scoring procedure used in quantifying departmental rankings was employed to translate the answers into numerical equivalents. As before, alternative systems of quantification produced only minor changes in rank order.

Before presenting the actual findings, we should repeat an earlier caveat. Table 13 reflects what the profession *believes* to be the relative weight of these attributes in contributing to personal success. These beliefs may not accurately represent the actual situation. Outside offers may turn altogether or in part on other considerations; or, even if these are the key attributes, they may operate in a manner quite at variance with popular understanding. But it is unlikely that grossly mistaken views would long endure on so sensitive and central a subject. And, to the extent that these perceptions are widely held, they influence behavior as well as thought and thus eventually tend to validate themselves.

---

[1] A number of other attributes were suggested—being a liberal, fellowship awards, governmental experience, active attendance at professional meetings, and the right background, to mention a few. The only one listed as many as a half-dozen times was personality.

THE TRIUMPH OF REALISM

Table 13 presents the manner in which political scientists rank the several attributes deemed instrumental in contributing to career success, defined as the ability to get outside offers.

TABLE 13

ATTRIBUTES CONTRIBUTING TO CAREER SUCCESS

Attribute	Rank	Score
Volume of publication	1	2.67
School at which doctorate was taken	2	2.58
Having the right connections	3	2.47
Ability to get research support	4	2.41
Quality of publication	5	2.22
Textbook authorship	6	2.15
Luck or chance	7	2.06
School of first full-time appointment	8	1.97
Self-promotion ("brass")	9	1.82
Teaching ability	10	1.29

The differential weights assigned to these ten items[2] hardly suggest, it must be confessed, the lofty standards and criteria expected of a learned discipline. They do not, in fact, put political science in a very favorable light. At this juncture an interesting question arises: Are political scientists a unique brand of academic

[2] Chi-square tests show the differences between all pairs of adjacent ranks except three to be statistically significant (P [Ho] < .05). The exceptions are 3 and 4, 6 and 7, and 7 and 8. However, the differences between 6 and 8 are highly significant (P [Ho] < .001). We have not stressed these results because statistical significance is a function of sample size. When pairs of adjacent ranks for all responses are analyzed, the number of cases becomes so large as to make even rather slight differences statistically significant.

man—that is, are their views on this subject influenced by their professional concern with and emphasis on the actuality rather than the mythology of who gets what, when, and how—or are these opinions also shared by the rest of the academic community? The problem is one to which we shall return.

Whatever the explanation, the three basic themes which run through the ordering in Table 13 plainly indicate a realistic rather than an idealistic conception of the factors which contribute to success. First, where *quality* comes into competition with *quantity* of publication, quality does not emerge triumphant. Second, personal and institutional connections play a major role in whether one gets ahead. Third, teaching ability has little, if any, bearing on advancement. Since the last generalization is the least novel of the three, we will dispose of it first and then take up the other two.

Teaching versus Research

Political scientists are clearly aware that "they are, in essence, paid to do one job, whereas the worth of their services is evaluated on the basis of how well they do another."[3] Although the great majority of them earn their living as teachers, pedagogical ability is rated as the least useful of the ten attributes in attracting outside offers. To be sure, it helps somewhat in advancement at home, but even here, as we shall see in the next chapter, "publish or perish" still controls promotion at many, many institutions, collegiate as well as graduate.

So much has been written on this topic that we need not treat it at length.[4] Knowledge of the low return from good teaching is passed from one academic generation to another more by example than by precept. An astute student, observing the manner in which his professors divide their energies between teaching and research and their efforts to reduce the former in order to devote

[3] Caplow and McGee, *op. cit.*, p. 82.
[4] Berelson, *op. cit.*, summarizes and comments on much of this literature.

additional time to the latter, quickly senses the relative value of the two in furthering his career.[5] For this reason, the recurrent complaint that our graduates are ill-equipped to serve as teachers misreads the situation. The problem is not the deficiency of their preparation but the working of a system which provides minimal rewards for instructoral excellence and devotion. A new Ph.D. is simply forced to choose between teaching and research—and this, as a sagacious critic has observed, is a choice between "almost incompatible occupations."[6] The ambitious academic obviously has little option in making this decision.

Publication: Quantity and Quality

The denigration of teaching, even by teachers, can be rationalized on the grounds that their primary responsibility is the discovery, rather than merely the transmission, of human knowledge. If so, publication, which is the final aspect of research, *should* be given precedence over teaching. Unfortunately, the force of this argument is somewhat lessened by the fact that quantity of publication (that is, of research) is ranked first—and quality fifth.

The importance attached to sheer volume of output[7] has elicited many expressions of dismay over the growing torrent of trivial research findings which see the light of day, and the comments from our respondents reflected the same concern. Still, none of the remedies proposed—boards of review, higher standards, and so on—actually comes to grips with the underlying problem. As long as quantity of publication is perceived as the controlling desideratum in professional advancement, it is utopian to expect a real change in a situation where "a great deal of foolish and unnecessary re-

[5] Orlans noted that "from 12 to 18 percent of university faculty in the arts and social sciences" now teach no undergraduates. *Op. cit.*, p. 48.

[6] Jacques Barzun, *The Teacher in America* (Boston: Little, Brown & Co., 1946), p. 202.

[7] This was epitomized by a note from one of our respondents in which he described how his chairman, an eminent political scientist now happily retired, would weigh the merits of rival job applicants by the "heft" of their publications in his hand.

search is undertaken by men who bring to their investigations neither talent nor interest."[8]

Item 6 of Table 13 was used to ascertain whether political scientists draw a sharp distinction, as some disciplines do, between the writing of textbooks and original research, with the former regarded as intellectually less demanding and hence less prestigious than the latter. The difference in kudos between the two seems to be very slight, a finding which may be of some practical value to those torn between the putative monetary rewards of "textcraft" and the desire to enhance their professional image.

Connections

The *Realpolitik* theme is sounded again when we look at the second-, third-, and eighth-ranked items. All of these can be subsumed by the term "connections," and the fourth-rated "ability to get research support" is susceptible to the same interpretation.

We earlier presented some data bearing on the relationship between school of doctoral origin and the type of academic appointments attained. The great importance attached by the profession to having the "right" degree makes it clear that a substantial segment of the membership is persuaded that many departments pursue a deliberate policy of favoring political scientists who have socially acceptable doctoral credentials. Much of the significance of the "school of first full-time appointment" item stems from this practice. Calls to prestigious departments come much more readily to persons already well situated than to those at humbler institutions. And, as we have seen, the better initial appointments are largely monopolized by Ph.D.'s trained at a small minority of departments. In the academic world, as elsewhere, "them which has, gets."

All that is implicit in the foregoing is symbolized by the attribute ranked third—"having the right connections." This phrase has many connotations, some fairly obvious, others on which we can only speculate. But the comments which accompanied the actual

[8] Caplow and McGee, *op. cit.*, p. 221.

ratings made it clear that the term was seen to relate to institutional origins; to influential sponsorship; to being strategically located in the discipline's communications network (or having a mentor so placed); to friendly relations with, if not actual membership in, the Establishment; and to useful contacts with foundations and governmental agencies.

Given the weight assigned to the several items falling within the connections syndrome, the respondents quite understandably felt that self-promotion has less bearing on career success than any other trait besides teaching ability. Their reasoning, in all probability, is that self-promotion is not likely to be very helpful unless one has the right connections and that, if one has these, self-promotion, in the aggressive and cruder sense signified by the word "brass," is hardly necessary.

MAJOR VARIABLES AND PERCEPTIONS OF WHO GETS WHAT

Up to this point we have described the collective views of the profession as they relate to the attributes which contribute to career success or failure, defined as the ability to attract outside offers. Needless to say, we expected that various subgroups in the discipline would perceive these attributes in a fashion somewhat different from both the membership at large and from that of one another. This expectation went largely unfulfilled. Perceptions of who gets what and how, are almost entirely independent of field commitment and of stand on the factors of behavioralism and the adequacy of the profession.

For example, the seven fields differed by no more than two ranks on all items except source of Ph.D. (two and one-half ranks), school of first full-time appointment (three ranks), and quality of publication (six ranks). The last is particularly interesting—public administration thought it second only to volume, but international relations and political theory placed it seventh and eighth, respectively. The extremes on the behavioralism factor were separated by more than two ranks only on scores for connections (three ranks) and on quality of publication (six ranks). Antibehavioralists rated connections second and quality ninth; their opposites put quality third and connections fifth.

The group believing the profession most adequate differed by more than two ranks from those thinking it least adequate only on the items dealing with research support and quality of publication (three ranks each). As one might have guessed, the former rank quality higher and research support lower than do the latter. The high-adequacy contingent rates quality third and research support fifth; the low-adequacy group gives quality sixth, and research support second, place.

All in all, however, the differences are far fewer than the similarities. Not only do the patterns of rank orderings by field and by extreme scores on the two factors reveal a basic communality of perceptions, but the distributions of responses to the individual items also show such slight variations that, in the final analysis, they must be treated as casual rather than causal.[9]

IMPLICATIONS

Since we are serving here primarily as *rapporteurs* and analysts rather than critics, it is not our responsibility or function to pass judgment on the views expressed. Nor are we obligated to express the pious hope that the respondents have badly mistaken the situation and that success turns far more on merit and true scholarly achievement than their answers suggest. We need speak, then, only to the subject—the data themselves.

[9] Differences in rank order were analyzed by the Kruskal-Wallis one-way analysis of variance for the seven fields and the Mann-Whitney U test for the extreme groups on each of the two factors. Differences in the distributions of responses to a given item were determined by the chi-square test for k independent samples. None of the rank order arrays proved statistically significant. Hardly more of the patterns of responses to particular items turned out significant than chance would have led one to expect. For example, the groups with highest and lowest scores on behavioralism differed to a significant degree (P [Ho] < .05) on only two items (quality of publication scores and self-promotion); the groups with highest and lowest scores on adequacy of the profession also differed on only two items (research support and teaching).

There can be no question that the three themes identified—the subordination of teaching to publication, the emphasis on quantity rather than quality of output, and the vital role of connections in career success—denote a frame of mind which, according to one's preference, can be called either realistic or cynical. What is not clear is whether this outlook is peculiar to political scientists and is the product of a special professional orientation or whether the views expressed are endemic in the academic community. If the latter is so, the matter goes far beyond the boundaries of our own discipline and becomes one of grave concern for the other learned disciplines as well.

To be sure, the existence of such an outlook has been frequently suggested in the literature dealing with American higher education —by Barzun, Riesman, Berelson, Caplow and McGee, and Sibley, to mention some of the more recent commentators. But the data heretofore adduced in support of the theory have been impressionistic rather than systematic. As far as we know, ours has been the first attempt to bring together, in an organized fashion, the perceptions of a discipline on this subject. Until comparative data are available, the question of whether political scientists are inherently different from other professions in this respect must remain unresolved. When one considers, though, the current proliferation of writing on the organization man, the "operator," and the way to succeed without really trying, it does seem unlikely that we shall emerge as atypical.

-9-

The Journals

Political scientists see publication as the most important single factor contributing to professional advancement, a belief probably shared with the larger academic community. For a fortunate minority this means the authorship of a book or monograph; for the majority it means, more realistically, an article in one of the scholarly journals.[1] Since there are many periodicals in which political scientists may and do publish, the query, "How do these journals compare in status?" is of practical concern, as well as of theoretical interest, to the student of the discipline. Stated less ele-

---

[1] Two studies, one of social scientists generally, the second of political scientists specifically, concluded that perhaps one out of three academicians will publish a book, rather generously defined, during the course of his career. See Paul F. Lazarsfeld and Wagner Thielens, Jr., *The Academic Mind* (Glencoe, Ill.: Free Press, 1958), p. 8, and V. O. Key, "The State of the Discipline," *American Political Science Review,* LII, No. 4 (1958), p. 970.

gantly, the question becomes "What is the prestige payoff of having an article appear in one periodical vis-à-vis another?"

Admittedly, prestige is a protean concept. To treat the subject adequately would require a far lengthier discussion of the ramifications of scholarly publication than is either possible or desirable here. Undoubtedly, many persons are motivated by considerations only indirectly, if at all, related to improving their marketability. Some seek enhanced prestige at their home institutions. A few may want an article accepted primarily for the satisfaction of proving to themselves that they are full-fledged masters of their craft. And others, aware that publication alone truly legitimizes research findings and gives the imprimatur of professional respectability to a new idea or approach, are most concerned with attaining intellectual recognition from their peers.

Whatever the individual imperative, academic man knows that the journals serving his discipline enjoy varying degrees of prestige.[2] To determine just how political scientists rate some of their leading scholarly periodicals, we asked, "To what extent do you think that publication in each of the following journals contributes to professional prestige in political science?" Pretest comment resulted in minor revision of the original list, and the final roster contained eleven journals—ten identified by name, and one, law reviews, by class. Five options were offered—"great deal," "some," "very little," "not at all," and "can't say" (Item C-5). Space was provided for additional entries if the rater felt that other journals should have been included.

Although the respondents added many other titles, only four received more than isolated mention. *Foreign Affairs* was nominated by some twenty persons, and the *Annals, Behavioral Science,* and the *Journal of Conflict Resolution* by about a half-dozen apiece. Some of the other journals proposed were *State Government, National Municipal Review, The New Yorker, Journal of Farm Economics, The Reporter,* and *International Organization.* Occasional references were also made to professional periodicals in psychology, sociology, and history.

---

[2] Only one respondent ventured to object that prestige "depends on the quality of the article, rather than the journal in which it appears."

The list of journals included in the questionnaire was deliberately limited to American publications, a decision to which very few of either the pretest panelists or the actual sample members took exception. Whether our inquiry was seen as dealing exclusively with American publications or whether the failure to voice objection to our bias reflects the parochialism of outlook which some observers have attributed to American political scientists is a matter of conjecture.

Three generalizations emerged from our data: (1) institutional pressures for "scholarship" are so great that there is *some* prestige to be gained from appearing even in the least highly regarded of the journals; (2) taking the profession as a whole, there is a clearly demarcated three-class hierarchy of journals, with definite prestige gradations between the classes; and (3) that, although there are noticeable differences among the various subgroups of political scientists in their perceptions of some of the journals, the ratings more often than not indicate an underlying consensus.

THE PRESTIGE OF PUBLICATION

The necessity of appearing in print and the benefits derived from almost any type of publication have already been suggested by the widespread belief that quantity of output is the first, and quality merely the fifth, most important element contributing to professional advancement. Fearful that we might be unaware of the situation or, perhaps, simply wishing to unburden themselves, many of the respondents described the demand at their institutions for "productive scholarship," a pressure no less unrelenting at many undergraduate colleges where good teaching is ostensibly the central concern than it is at the graduate departments which make no pretense about the matter. Comments contained repeated mention of the need for additional journal outlets, several versions of the "publish or perish" aphorism, and one bitter complaint that, at the respondent's school, "even the mediocre have to publish to be promoted."

But the most persuasive evidence of the prestige attached to almost any publication emerges from the ratings themselves. These are given in Table 14.

TABLE 14

CONTRIBUTIONS TO PROFESSIONAL PRESTIGE IN POLITICAL
SCIENCE OF PUBLICATION IN VARIOUS JOURNALS

Number of Responses

Journal	A great deal	Some	Very little	Not at all	Can't say*	Total
Administrative Science Quarterly	41	178	35	2	175	431
American Behavioral Scientist	32	160	85	12	142	431
American Political Science Review	321	75	6	—	29	431
Journal of Politics	137	221	19	1	53	431
Midwest Journal of Political Science	35	232	64	4	96	431
Political Science Quarterly	95	212	56	6	62	431
Public Administration Review	78	172	56	13	112	431
Public Opinion Quarterly	48	195	59	6	123	431
Western Political Quarterly	61	226	52	4	88	431
World Politics	138	144	32	2	115	431

* Includes failure to check any option.

There were over three thousand specific journal evaluations. Although almost everybody rated the *Review*, the number of "can't says" and blank answers increased sharply at the lower reaches of the hierarchy. For the ten named periodicals, 85 per cent of the ratings fell into either the "a great deal" or "some" categories;

barely 15 per cent were at either of the two lower levels. More to the point, there were only fifty "not at all" gradings, less than 2 per cent of the total, and half of these were concentrated on a pair of journals. Even the least esteemed periodical received one or the other of the two highest evaluations from two-thirds of its graders. The generosity with which prestige was attributed would seem less remarkable if all journals were regarded as standing on the same plane, but this is not the case. There can be little doubt that the compulsion for publication has created a situation where, as one respondent wryly observed, "*Any* journal helps some."

THE STATUS HIERARCHY OF JOURNALS

Although every professional journal endows its contributors with a measure of praise, some are clearly more prestigious than others. The ratings for each journal were quantified by the same technique employed when dealing with departmental rankings (Chapter 4), and, as in that instance, prestige index scores were computed. When this statistical device is applied, the ten journals fall into three categories.

Perhaps the two most striking aspects of this ranking are the gulf between the *American Political Science Review* and all the other journals and the narrow spread of index scores among the periodicals in the two lower categories.

Though hardly unexpected, the pre-eminence of the *Review* is emphasized by the manner in which it outdistanced its nearest rivals. For example, 80 per cent of the raters said that the *Review* carried a great deal of prestige; little more than half thought this was true of the next ranking journals. In a way, this margin of superiority is a bit startling. We earlier noted that almost one-third of those taking a stand on the matter thought that the quality of articles currently published in the *Review* does not compare favorably with those published prior to 1945 (Table 1, Item 10). This view may be only a manifestation of a nostalgic "good old days" sentiment. Still, the apparent discrepancy between the two sets of judgments hints that the *Review*'s massive prestige does not stem

TABLE 15

PRESTIGE RANKING OF POLITICAL SCIENCE JOURNALS

Journal	Index score
A Most prestigious	
American Political Science Review	2.78
B Considerable prestige	
World Politics	2.32
Journal of Politics	2.31
C Less prestigious	
Political Science Quarterly	2.07
Administrative Science Quarterly	2.01
Western Political Quarterly	2.00
Public Administration Review	1.99
Public Opinion Quarterly	1.93
Midwest Journal of Politics	1.89
American Behavioral Scientist	1.73

entirely from a regard for the quality of its contents but is in some measure a product of its role as the official organ—with its correspondingly higher circulation—of the national Association.[3] The general tenor of comments volunteered by the respondents, we might add, supports this supposition.[4]

Below the *Review* there is, in effect, a tie for second place between *World Politics* and *Journal of Politics,* with scores almost exactly midway between those of the journals immediately above

[3] We do not know the degree to which this consideration may have influenced the ratings of journals which serve as the organs of regional associations—for example, *Journal of Politics, Western Political Quarterly,* and so on. Our respondents were not asked to indicate the geographical location of their present position and, although this was not an insurmountable difficulty, we did not think that the end product warranted the effort.

[4] The language employed on this subject made up in vigor what it lacked in dispassion. It was exceeded in virulence, we would say, only by the comments directed to the competence, judgment, and taste of the authors of this study.

and below them. Although the less prestigious group includes seven titles, only .18 points separates the fourth- from the ninth-ranked journal, and only .08 points divides fourth from seventh position. These differences are not so small that they warrant the conclusion that the profession sees the periodicals in this classification as essentially equal in status. On the other hand, neither are they so great as to mandate a further subdivision of category.[5]

The ranking in Table 15 is based on all responses and therefore represents the over-all evaluation of the profession. With this consensus as a point of departure, we can now examine the manner in which subgroups in the discipline assess these periodicals.

THE VARIABLES OF JOURNAL PRESTIGE

Table 16 summarizes the impact of our standard three variables—field of specialization and the factors of behavioralism and the adequacy of the profession.

Before turning to some of the details, we might glance at the unweighted average scores. These make possible a very crude comparison of the amount of prestige attributed to journal publication by each of the designated groups. This measure indicates that the most generous in their attribution of prestige are those who regard

[5] Statistical difference between the patterning of responses for each pair of journals was determined by means of the chi-square distribution. The infrequency of "not at all" responses led us to combine them with those in the "very little" category in making these computations. Two problems, rather commonly experienced with the chi-square test, make us reluctant to give a great deal of weight to these results. The first of these problems was referred to in Chapter 8, note 2—when a large number of cases is involved, even small differences tend to be statistically significant. Second and even more important, statistical significance can be reached as a result of differences of conflicting character. For example, the differences in patterning between the rating options selected for *World Politics* and *Journal of Politics* are statistically significant at the .001 level of confidence. But the direction of these differences is ambiguous. The large chi square is caused by a combination of higher than expected ratings for *World Politics* in both the "great deal" and "little/not at all" cells; lower than expected ratings for *World Politics* in the "some" cell; higher than expected ratings for the *Journal* in the "some" cell; and lower than expected ratings for the *Journal* in the "great deal" and "little/not at all" cells.

the profession as especially adequate and those who are in the fields of American government, general politics, public administration, and public law. The most niggardly in this respect are the political scientists who view the discipline as particularly inadequate, those who are antibehavioral in orientation, and those who are in political theory and international relations.

Field Affiliations and Journal Prestige

Differences among the several fields in perceptions of journal prestige may be quite readily traced in Table 16. The specialized journals in particular are viewed quite differently by persons in the several fields. Nevertheless, careful inspection reveals an underlying consensus which is confirmed by statistical analysis.[6] However field affiliations affect assessments of the specialized journals, they do not produce a departure from the over-all rating pattern. Perhaps the best way to see this is first to deal with the *Review,* since it is *sui generis,* and then to examine the relationship between field affiliation and rankings of the other journals.

Although 80 per cent of those who gave a specific rating to the *Review* selected the most prestigious option offered, perceptions are not entirely independent of the field of the rater. The *Review* enjoys the greatest standing among those in public law (2.92) and comparative government (2.88) and the least among those in political theory (2.71) and international relations (2.70). Despite these differentials, it is the first-place choice for all seven fields.

All the other journals are affected to some extent by variations related to field membership, although not enormously so. The two which suffer least from field-related fluctuations are *Journal of Politics* and *American Behavioral Scientist.* If journal index scores are ordered by rank within each field, *Journal of Politics* in every instance receives a second or a third place; and *ABS,* a ninth or tenth position. *World Politics* is only somewhat more volatile, with five of the seven fields giving it a second or a third place. The two

[6] The Kruskal-Wallis one-way analysis of variance was used for this purpose.

TABLE 16

VARIABLES AFFECTING PERCEPTIONS OF JOURNAL PRESTIGE

Journal	Over-all	Index score by fields			
		Int. rel.	Comp. govt.	Pub. law	Polit. theory
American Political Science Review	2.78	2.70	2.88	2.92	2.71
World Politics	2.32	2.59	2.43	2.18	2.13
Journal of Politics	2.31	2.22	2.29	2.51	2.26
Political Science Quarterly	2.07	2.10	2.13	2.08	2.09
Administrative Science Quarterly	2.01	1.86	2.00	1.92	1.81
Western Political Quarterly	2.00	1.84	2.05	2.22	1.95
Public Administration Review	1.99	1.80	2.03	1.90	1.94
Public Opinion Quarterly	1.93	1.89	1.89	1.88	1.84
Midwest Journal of Political Science	1.89	1.73	1.70	2.06	1.85
American Behavioral Scientist	1.73	1.76	1.67	1.77	1.52
Unweighted average	2.10	2.05	2.11	2.14	2.01

$H = 2.20$

$P\ (Ho) > .05$

TABLE 16

(CONTINUED)

Index score by factors

Pub. admin.	Amer. govt.	Gen. pol.	Pro-behavioral	Anti-behavioral	More adequate	Less adequate
2.80	2.79	2.83	2.86	2.70	2.84	2.78
2.15	2.29	2.24	2.41	2.29	2.36	2.26
2.29	2.34	2.30	2.29	2.29	2.34	2.22
2.28	1.95	1.97	1.83	2.13	2.25	1.83
2.18	2.10	2.14	2.19	1.76	1.95	2.00
1.95	2.07	2.08	1.94	2.10	2.05	1.88
2.18	2.12	1.92	1.74	2.07	2.24	1.85
1.95	2.00	2.10	2.06	1.62	1.81	1.81
1.84	2.02	2.10	1.91	1.83	1.94	1.74
1.74	1.83	1.72	1.84	1.52	1.57	1.70
2.14	2.15	2.14	2.11	2.03	2.14	2.01

$$U = 44.5 \qquad U = 34.5$$

$$P (Ho) > .05 \qquad P (Ho) > .05$$

exceptions are public law and public administration, which rank *World Politics* fourth and sixth, respectively.

A rough indication of the extent to which specialized journals are favored by the fields they serve may be gleaned from the magnitude of the index scores. *World Politics* receives especially high ratings from those in international relations and comparative government; *Public Administration Review* and *Administrative Science Quarterly*, from those in administration; and *Public Opinion Quarterly*, from those in general politics and processes. However, what may be most worthy of emphasis is not that field commitments tend to color political scientists' perceptions of journals, but that these filters do not stop them from seeing the matter in essentially a common light.

Behavioralism and Adequacy of the Profession

Like field identification, strong commitments on either behavioralism or adequacy of the profession are not entirely independent of perceptions of journal prestige. Table 16 also presents the journal prestige index scores for the persons taking more extreme positions on each factor.

If we order these scores by rank, no more than one position separates the assessments of the most and the least behaviorally oriented on five publications—*American Political Science Review, World Politics, Journal of Politics, Western Political Quarterly,* and *Midwest Journal.* The widest disagreement occurs over *Political Science Quarterly,* which the probehavioralists rank ninth and the antibehavioralists fourth. The behaviorally committed also consider *Administrative Science Quarterly, Public Opinion Quarterly,* and *American Behavioral Scientist* more prestigious and *Public Administration Review* less prestigious than the antibehavioralists.

When the factor of adequacy of the profession is introduced, no more than a single place divides the two factions on seven journals—that is, all but *Political Science Quarterly, Midwest Journal,* and *Administrative Science Quarterly.* Of the three the first two are more highly regarded by those who consider the discipline adequate and the third by those who do not.

There is enough agreement on rank ordering so that the overall perceptions of the ultras on each factor must be regarded as essentially similar. But it does not necessarily follow that the differences in perceptions of particular journals may be readily attributed to chance. On the contrary, those in sharpest contention over behavioralism disagree to a statistically significant extent on five journals—*American Political Science Review, Political Science Quarterly, Western Political Quarterly, Administrative Science Quarterly, Public Opinion Quarterly*—and the extremists on the adequacy factor disagree on three—*Political Science Quarterly, Public Administration Review, Midwest Journal*.[7] When all is given its due, it seems to us that consensus dominates conflict.

The "Old School Tie" and Journal Prestige

On a couple of occasions we have discussed the halo effect and its influence on rankings and perceptions. The "old school tie" is simply a variant of this phenomenon.

Three of the journals listed have especially close bonds with a given university—*World Politics* with Princeton; *Political Science Quarterly* with Columbia; and *Administrative Science Quarterly* with Cornell. The small number of Cornell Ph.D.'s in our sample, mirroring that university's modest doctoral output, limited our inquiry to the first two mentioned periodicals. Our findings were so striking that we decided they would make a fitting note on which to conclude this chapter.

Princetonians give *World Politics* a score of 2.69, well above the rest of the profession's 2.31. Columbians rated *Political Science Quarterly* at 2.33, a goodly distance above the 2.06 earned from political scientists in general. But the two chauvinisms are not cut entirely from the same cloth. Columbia Ph.D.'s scored *World*

[7] Chi-square tests were used for this purpose. The limitations set forth in note 5 are not serious problems here.

Politics at a generous 2.52, whereas Princetonians rated *Political Science Quarterly* a scornful 1.78. Princeton Ph.D.'s also take a rather cavalier attitude toward the *Review* (2.67), whereas the 2.78 for Columbia Ph.D.'s was exactly in line with the profession at large. The responses afford an interesting, if, to the *cognoscenti*, not unexpected, example of institutional ethnocentricism.

-10-
The Establishment

American political scientists have long employed power and influence as key analytical constructs. It is only fitting, therefore, that this study devote some attention to their perceptions of an institution frequently alleged to exercise influence and power over the management of their own profession. We refer, of course, to the Establishment.

Like Parkinson's constantly proliferating laws, the concept of the Establishment is a British contribution to contemporary social science. And, like Parkinson's formulations, it is sufficiently lacking in precision so that it can be bent to a variety of purposes. As even a casual study of the literature reveals, the term "Establishment" has been used with equal facility to refer to anything from a ruling oligarchy of identifiable dimensions to a potpourri of families, officeholders, "influentials," taste-makers, court jesters, and et ceteras.[1] But our interest here is neither in this literature nor in the semantics of the matter. What concerns us, rather, is: (1) How substantial a segment of American political science believes that an Establishment plays a significant role in the affairs of their discipline?[2] and (2) What relationship is there between perceptions of the Establishment and opinions held on other issues?

These two questions fixed the boundaries for this phase of our inquiry. A number of respondents, many of whom manifestly had strong feelings on the subject, complained that we failed to identify other areas in which an Establishment, as they saw it, was clearly operative—control over Association elections, access to research funds, and publication in the professional journals. Here we must plead guilty.

IS THERE AN ESTABLISHMENT?

Two of the twenty-six statements in Part B of the questionnaire were specifically designed to develop data on whether political scientists think there is an influential Establishment in the profession. These were Items 16 and 26, and the responses were as in Table 17.

Brief attention to the wording of these statements, as well as to the results, may be instructive.

Item 16 is general in nature—"American political science has developed an Establishment which largely determines the character and standards of the discipline." A person could disagree or strongly disagree with this formulation for one of two totally different rea-

---

[1] Some of the more exotic items of this literature are cited in the footnotes to Richard H. Rovere's essay, "The American Establishment," in *The American Establishment* (New York: Harcourt, Brace & World, Inc.), 1962, pp. 3–21. Rovere subjected many of these materials to rigorous analysis but erred, in our opinion, in not fully utilizing the Gilbert-Sullivan multivocal coefficient of credibility.

[2] For convenience of discussion, we shall speak of "the" or "an" Establishment. As one of our respondents observed, however, it is quite possible that "there is not one but several Establishments, each with its own sphere of influence."

TABLE 17

RESPONSES ON ESTABLISHMENT STATEMENTS

		Percentage of respondents indicating			
Statement	Strongly agree	Agree	Can't say	Disagree	Strongly disagree
16	10.0	36.0	25.3	26.7	2.1
26	14.4	27.6	45.9	10.2	1.9

sons. He might do so because he feels that there is no Establishment in American political science or, alternatively, because he believes that an Establishment exists, but that it is not particularly effective in this area. Similar, if more complex, ambiguities underlie the "can't say" replies. On the other hand, the "agree" and "strongly agree" answers are unambiguous. For a respondent to select either of these options, he had to think both that an Establishment exists and that it is influential. Note that almost half (46.0 per cent) of those who answered this question go along with the fairly sweeping contentions in this item.

Statement 26 is much more specific—"There has developed an inner group in the American Political Science Association which, in large part, controls the key panel assignments at the annual Association meetings." This item would be expected to have salience primarily for those members of the profession experienced with and interested in panel assignments. The responses lend support to this expectation since the proportion of "can't says" almost doubles. Nevertheless, the total percentage of "strongly agree" and "agree" is not much below that recorded for Item 16.

When the two sets of answers are cross-tabulated, we find that 58.9 per cent of all respondents checked an "agree" or "strongly agree" option at least once, whereas only 7.2 per cent "disagreed" or "strongly disagreed" with both statements. Undoubtedly, a sizable majority of political scientists perceives the existence of an

Establishment which wields substantial influence over at least some aspects of professional life. Moreover, as the write-in comments pointed out, we did not deal with other areas in which an Establishment is also thought to be operative. Had we touched on these, an even larger proportion of respondents probably would have disclosed positive perceptions of a powerful Establishment.

VARIABLES RELATING TO PERCEPTIONS OF ESTABLISHMENT

As indicated in Chapter 3 when discussing behavioralism and the adequacy of the profession, a third factor appeared no matter what subgroups were analyzed. This factor, the smallest of the three in its ability to account for the variance in the twenty-six statements, loaded heavily on Items 16 and 26 but on no others. For obvious reasons we have termed it the "Establishment factor." The same procedures were used in computing the Establishment factor score for each respondent as for the two larger factors.

Because only two items were involved, the distribution of the profession on this factor does not require a chart. Of the twenty-five scores possible, only four were needed to represent the answers of 60 per cent of the respondents to these statements. These four result from the weights given the following combinations of entries: "agree" to both statements; "can't say" to both; "agree" to Item 16 and "can't say" to 26; and "disagree" to 16 and "can't say" to 26. No other combination was resorted to by as many as 6 per cent of the respondents.

When factor scores for all respondents are plotted, the resulting distribution tends to resemble a normal curve to a greater extent than does the distribution on either of the larger factors. As the four most frequent combinations suggest and as reflected in the fact that almost 60 per cent of the respondents agreed at least once, there is an unmistakable skewing toward the higher perception end of the continuum.

Establishment and Field of Specialization

Field of specialization has frequently colored the respondents' views on intellectual and professional issues, as noted in a number of instances. This is much less the case on the Establishment factor. With a single exception all fields take essentially the same position. The nonconformists, oddly enough, are those in public administration, who tend to be rather skeptical of the existence of a powerful Establishment. We say "oddly enough" because those in this field, as specialists on organizations, should be the most discerning about this phenomenon. Why should persons presumably so knowledgeable about organizational matters show the lowest perception of Establishment? Perhaps having lived on Loch Ness for so long, they are least convinced of the monster's reality.

The Establishment and Behavioralism and Adequacy of the Profession

The type of factor analysis used in this study (orthogonal simple structure) produced uncorrelated factors, but this does not preclude the possibility of sharp differences between the way in which extreme groups on a given factor view the other factors. In identifying the two groups holding the more extreme views on the Establishment, we employed the same methods used in dealing with the other factors (see Chapter 3). That is, persons whose factor scores exceed one standard deviation above the mean will be considered the "high-Establishment group" and those whose factor scores fall by more than this amount below the mean the "low-Establishment group."

This mode of analysis discloses that the possibility suggested above does, in fact, exist. The high-Establishment contingent is relatively antibehavioral in persuasion, whereas the low-Establishment element tends to be behaviorally oriented. The difference between the groups is highly significant statistically.

Contrary to the pattern just described, the opposing factions are almost identical in their assessments of the adequacy of the discipline. The means and standard deviations of their scores on the adequacy factor barely differ.

The Establishment and Views on How to Get Ahead

There are some striking disparities between the high- and the low-Establishment contingents in their appraisal of the attributes which contribute to career success.

TABLE 18

ESTABLISHMENT EXTREMES ON ATTRIBUTES CONTRIBUTING
TO PROFESSIONAL SUCCESS

	High-Estab't.		Low-Estab't.	
Attributes	Rank	Score	Rank	Score
Volume of publication	1	2.75	1	2.64
School at which doctorate was taken	4	2.52	3	2.38
Having the right connections	2	2.65	5	2.18
Ability to get research support	3	2.56	4	2.23
Quality of publication	8	1.96	2	2.51
Textbook authorship	5	2.34	8	1.86
Luck or chance	6	2.28	6	2.03
School of first full-time appointment	9	1.58	7	1.88
Self-promotion ("brass")	7	2.10	9	1.56
Teaching ability	10	1.15	10	1.51

$U = 37$

$P (Ho) > .05$

As the scores reveal, the high-Establishment respondents put greater emphasis on connections, the ability to get research sup-

port, and self-promotion; they give less weight to quality of publication and school of first full-time appointment. The variations
in the over-all rank ordering by the two groups do not quite
reach the required level of significance. However, despite the small
number of persons in each of these subsamples, the differences in
the two response patterns to each of the six attributes mentioned
do attain this level. The findings indicate a fairly persistent relationship between strong perceptions of the Establishment and notions
of who gets what and how.

ESTABLISHMENT: THE INS AND THE OUTS?

Political scientists who believe strongly in the existence of an
influential Establishment, to recapitulate, tend to be antibehavioral
in outlook and to see connections, brass, and the ability to get research money as relatively important in contributing to advancement within the discipline. Political scientists with opposing views
on the Establishment tend to be probehavioral and to regard quality
of publication as relatively more important in contributing to success. Can we somehow account for these two patterns of perception?

The simplest explanation is that of the ins and the outs. Since
those with a high perception of the Establishment are antibehavioral
in orientation, we might argue that they see the behavioralists as
presently dominating the profession and constituting the Establishment.[3] This would account for the relatively cynical fashion in
which they evaluate the attributes contributing to professional advancement today. From time immemorial, such has been the viewpoint of the outs. One could similarly account for the complex of
values held by those with low perceptions of the Establishment.
Probehavioralist in sympathies and thus more attuned to the Establishment, they would be more inclined either to deny its existence
or to grant it a very unimportant role. And, as they see it, success

[3] We do not want to imply that perception of the Establishment always coincides with hostility or opposition to it. At least a small number
believe, as one respondent rather tartly put it, "Of course there is an Establishment—and there should be!"

quite properly turns on true ability. From time immemorial, too, such has been the viewpoint of the ins.

To summarize: A very substantial percentage of the membership believes that there is an influential Establishment operative in certain areas of American political science; a relatively small minority denies this to be the case. Perceptions of the Establishment, high and low, associate strongly with opinions on behavioralism and how to get ahead. These two viewpoints, we have suggested, may be essentially those of the ins and the outs.

The purist may object that this reasoning relies on *petitio principii* to explain why the antibehavioralists are high in their perceptions of Establishment—and that it then compounds the felony by employing the argument *ad hominem* to account for the beliefs held by each camp. But these are purely logical objections and should not deter us from considering the theory on its merits.

-11-
The Have-Nots

Two of the most striking trends in American political science, as noted in Chapter 1, are the academization and the professionalization of the discipline. The former has progressed to the point where nearly three-quarters of the Association's membership presently hold appointments at institutions of higher learning; the latter, to where slightly more than 50 per cent of all members and 75 per cent of the academicians (those who teach at colleges and universities) currently possess earned doctorates.[1] As a result of these trends, the profession is now divided into three major segments. The largest, a bit over 55 per cent, is made up of academics who

---

[1] Based on sampling of the 1961 *Directory,* part-time teachers and student members of the Association excluded. For those of professorial rank (assistant, associate, and full), the figure is 80 per cent. The respondents to our questionnaire, as noted in Appendix A, tended to overrepresent the academic side of the profession.

hold a doctorate. The smallest, some 15 per cent, are the academics who do *not* have a doctorate. Between these two is the second minority, the almost 30 per cent of political scientists who earn their livings as other than educators and to whom we will henceforth refer as "nonacademics."

In our analyses thus far, no attempt has been made to distinguish between the beliefs and perceptions of these groups. The obvious thought—and it has undoubtedly already occurred to the reader—is whether the attitudes and views of the two minorities are the same as those of the main body of the profession. The present chapter is devoted to this question. We will first deal with the non-Ph.D. academic, then with the nonacademic political scientist.

THE NON-PH.D. ACADEMIC

The Problem of the Permanent Non-Ph.D.

If the non-Ph.D. academics were simply doctorates in the making, there would have been little reason to single them out for special treatment. In fact, we had not originally planned to devote a separate section to this topic. Rather, the decision grew out of the realization that many—perhaps even a majority—of the academic political scientists without doctorates will never attain the degree. They are, to put it bluntly, permanent non-Ph.D.'s in a learned discipline where these three letters have become a necessity for acceptance by professional peers and administrative superiors.

The evidence which led to this conclusion can be quickly summarized. For the social sciences in general and for political science in particular, the elapsed time between the baccalaurate and doctoral degrees is a shade under ten years.[2] The mean age on earning the doctorate is usually about thirty-two, though the figures may vary slightly from year to year.[3] For example, there were twenty-five respondents to the questionnaire who received

[2] Sibley, *op. cit.*, p. 100.
[3] Orlans, *op. cit.*, p. 117.

their degrees in 1961 and 1962 (that is, after the *Directory* data were compiled). Two-thirds were between twenty-five and thirty-five years old, and their average age when taking the degree was just over thirty-three. The basic pattern has repeated itself with enough consistency to warrant the inference that, if one has not achieved his doctorate before reaching thirty-five (to take a generous outer limit), the chances turn heavily against him.

Some 25 per cent of the full-time academics in the profession do not have doctorates. About 55 per cent of this group are over thirty-five years old. (Their average age, in fact, is over thirty-nine.) We must therefore conclude that a very sizable proportion of these non-Ph.D.'s will never attain doctorates, barring some drastic upheaval in the system of higher education. Actually, the foregoing is but a crude statistical exposition of a law about which most graduate faculties are intuitively aware—the longer a candidate takes, the less his chances of ultimate success. Beyond a certain point and age, the quest is increasingly doomed to frustration.

So much for a rather bleak generalization. Given the workings of the academic market place, a series of consequences might plausibly be expected to flow from this situation. First, the employment opportunities of the permanent non-Ph.D.'s should be more circumscribed than for persons with a doctorate. Second, their views on professional issues should differ from those of their fellow academicians because they tend to be further removed, by the nature of their appointments, from the main stream of professional activity. Finally, their status as an underprivileged minority should be reflected in their satisfaction—or lack thereof—with political science as a chosen vocation.

Since the conception of the permanent non-Ph.D. as a special problem did not develop until after we had begun to analyze our data, we made no specific provision in the original study design for identifying and isolating this group. To test the expectations stated above, we have consequently had to resort to some devices improvised, as it were, under the spur of necessity. Although these techniques are not always so elegant as might be desired, we do think that they are reasonably adequate for the purposes intended.

Restricted Career Opportunities

Everyone knows that non-Ph.D.'s have a limited range of employment possibilities in academia even though empiric documentation of this truism has not previously been provided for political science. Still, there may be a certain virtue in demonstrating the obvious. At the very worst, the undertaking establishes what is widely believed to be self-evident, and it occasionally leads to an unexpected insight.

We need hardly expatiate on the significance attached to the doctorate by most schools or on their reluctance to hire or retain faculty members who do not have or are not likely to attain this degree. An examination of the institutional affiliations of the non-Ph.D.'s now serving as full-time teachers reveals the extent to which the market place has, in the parlance of Wall Street, discounted their doctoral prospects. There were forty-seven such persons among our respondents. Three had appointments at one of the "top eleven" departments; six were at graduate departments in the lower half of the ranking; one was at a prestige college; and two held positions at "good" colleges. The remaining thirty-five were employed either at nonranked universities or at "other" colleges.

As the younger people in this group have a better statistical chance of getting their degrees, they might be expected to show a higher incidence of "better" appointments. But this is not the case. The pattern is basically unchanged even when the non-Ph.D.'s are split into those above and below thirty-five years old. Only when we take the third group mentioned above, those listed as non-Ph.D.'s in the 1961 *Directory* but who gained their degrees over the next two years, do we begin to approach the distribution of appointments which generally characterizes the profession (see Chapter 5). The explanation, in all probability, for the similarity in employment pattern between the older and the younger non-Ph.D.'s is that the more prestigious schools are not inclined to gamble, even on the more youthful candidates, in awarding tenure.

Consequently, the academic who lacks the doctorate must turn, fairly soon in his career, to the institutions with less exalted standards.

There is, of course, another factor operative. Sophisticated academicians are aware that taking a full-time teaching post before little is left to complete other than the finishing touches on the dissertation can be explained as an effect as well as a cause. Few good graduate departments today are unable to subsidize, by some device or another, the candidates regarded as really promising. For the most part, then, students who have to go into full-time teaching prior to reaching this point are those whose abilities are not highly esteemed by their mentors and whose professional prospects might not have been appreciably brighter even had they been able to continue their work without interruption.

In either event, the data suggest that there are three career patterns, each with its own employment potentials.[4] At one end of the scale, enjoying the widest scope of opportunity, are the academics who, in effect, go right through to their doctorates. Next, with a narrower range of options, come those who receive their degrees only after an intervening period of full-time teaching. Finally, at the opposite end of the scale, with the most drastically restricted prospects, are the academics permanently without a Ph.D.

Stand on Intellectual Issues

With careers that take them primarily into undergraduate teaching at the less renowned colleges, the permanent non-Ph.D.'s are farther removed from the main stream of professional life than their colleagues at the universities and the "better" undergraduate institutions. In theory, they should be able to keep up with developments through journals, monographs, and attendance at the Association's national and regional meetings. Is this actually the case?

[4] For purposes of this discussion, we have treated all doctorates as equal. Since, in reality, this is not the case, at least a sixfold classification would be needed to describe the situation more accurately.

Are they equally familiar with the intellectual issues before the profession? Are their views on these issues the same as those of other academic members of the discipline?

Before we can tackle these questions, we must decide just who is to be compared with whom. There are a number of obvious pairings—all Ph.D.'s with all non-Ph.D.'s; the younger (below thirty-five) with the older non-Ph.D.'s; the older non-Ph.D.'s with the older Ph.D.'s. The last of these, we would say, affords the best basis for comparison. A large majority of the permanent nondoctorates would certainly be in this age bracket, and their Ph.D. contemporaries would be the persons, degrees aside, with whom they would presumably have the most in common. The following analysis, then, is based on these two groups.

To measure familiarity—more precisely, declared familiarity—with current professional issues, we developed an "index of nonfamiliarity." This index simply describes the frequency with which a respondent or class of respondents resorted to "can't say" answers on the twenty-six statements in Part B of the questionnaire. For the older Ph.D. academics the index score is 3.61; for the counterpart non-Ph.D.'s it is 6.08. Although the difference between the two scores is not overwhelming, it does lend modest support to the proposition that, in this respect, the permanent non-Ph.D. stands somewhat apart from his colleagues.[5]

Little difference exists between the two groups on the three major factors. The permanent non-Ph.D.'s are slightly more hostile to behavioralism; they are somewhat more sanguine about the adequacy of the profession; and they tend to have a higher perception of the Establishment. None of the variations, however, approach the required level of statistical significance.[6]

[5] If "can't say" and other than "can't say" responses are compared for the two groups, the chi-square test shows this to be statistically significant (P [Ho] < .001), but Fisher's T test for the difference between uncorrelated proportions does not (P [Ho] > .05). On the whole, we tend to feel that the Fisher T is somewhat more appropriate in these circumstances, hence the cautious tone of the text.

[6] As in earlier chapters, t tests were used to determine the statistical significance between the responses of two groups to each of the twenty-six items in Part B of the questionnaire.

Many of the twenty-six statements are not closely associated with any of the major factors. Three of these statements (5, 13, and 18) deal with the strengths and weaknesses of existing doctoral programs. Here, if anywhere, one would expect the non-Ph.D.'s to differ in outlook. Such is the case, for they are much more critical on all three than are the Ph.D.'s. Further comment would be superfluous.

On only one other statement (11) do the differences between the two groups reach the conventional required level of significance (P [Ho] < .05). We would be tempted to dismiss this as a casual occurrence were it not for two considerations. First, the statement deals with the impact of nonscholarly activities on the development of the discipline, and it is the non-Ph.D.'s who are least convinced that these activities are injurious. Second, on the one other item related to nonscholarly activity (Item 19, which asks whether political scientists devote enough attention to public policy matters), the scores again varied in the same direction and failed to attain statistical significance by only a thin margin ($t = 1.80$).

The foregoing differences between the attitudes of the Ph.D.'s and non-Ph.D.'s thirty-five and above in age occur on those few issues where, if anywhere, the two groups would be expected to have opposed perceptions. By and large, the permanent non-Ph.D.'s do not have a unique perspective on the intellectual issues before the profession. On three-quarters of the statements their responses indicate that they share with the Ph.D.'s a common body of beliefs and values. It is hard to escape the conclusion that the similarities between the two are much greater than the dissimilarities.

Views on Who Gets What How

The academic non-Ph.D. is not only a member of a minority group but of a grossly underprivileged minority in terms of opportunity for advancement at home and freedom to move to other schools. Promotion, salary, and mobility inevitably are matters of intense personal concern, and even the most unworldly non-Ph.D. can hardly be unaware of the handicaps inherent in his special

status. We were fairly confident, therefore, that ratings given by
this group to the ten attributes contributing to professional advancement would vary from those made by fellow political scientists
(also thirty-five and over) possessing the indispensable doctorate.
This confidence was largely misplaced, as can be seen from the following table. The items are listed in the order of importance attributed to them by the profession at large (see Table 13).

TABLE 19

ATTRIBUTES CONTRIBUTING TO OUTSIDE JOB OFFERS:
PERCEPTIONS OF ACADEMIC PH.D.'S AND ACADEMIC
NON-PH.D.'S BORN IN 1927 OR BEFORE

| | Non-Ph.D.'s | | Ph.D.'s | |
Attribute	Rank	Score	Rank	Score
Volume of publication	1	2.68	1	2.68
School at which doctorate was taken	2	2.50	2	2.50
Having the right connections	3	2.40	4	2.45
Ability to get research support	9	1.76	3	2.46
Quality of publication	8	1.81	5	2.27
Textbook authorship	4	2.36	6	2.15
Luck or chance	5	2.15	7	2.05
School of first full-time appointment	6	2.05	8	1.95
Self-promotion ("brass")	7	2.00	9	1.80
Teaching ability	10	1.18	10	1.28

$U = 44$
$P (Ho) > .05$
$Tau = .56$

On two attributes, volume of publication and source of doctorate, scores as well as rank are identical. A third, teaching ability,
is assigned the same position by both groups. The greatest single
divergence is on research support (six ranks); next is quality of
publication (three ranks). On all the others the difference is two

ranks or less. Compared with similar tables previously examined, the differentials in magnitude of scores seem quite large on a number of items. Actually, because of the small size of the non-Ph.D. sample, only that on quality of publication reaches significance. When the whole array is statistically analyzed, the basic similarity in outlook between the permanent non-Ph.D.'s and the Ph.D.'s of the same age is again confirmed.[7]

Career Satisfaction

How satisfied are the permanent non-Ph.D.'s with their choice of career? Considering their anomalous status in a learned discipline, it is no shock to find that they manifest, at best, restrained enthusiasm when asked whether they would make the same choice of profession if they had it to do all over again. Almost 20 per cent gave either a "definitely not" or "probably not" answer; less than 25 per cent said "definitely yes." Comparable figures for the Ph.D. group are "definitely not" or "probably not," 15 per cent; "definitely yes," 40 per cent. That the non-Ph.D.'s should be relatively unhappy with their lot is hardly surprising; that the margin of dissatisfaction should be so small perhaps is.

This brings us to an issue the outlines of which have become increasingly visible over the past few pages. Accepted dogma holds that there is a profound gap in scholarly ability and knowledge between those who have and those who do not have the doctorate. In fact, the overriding importance attached to the degree must rest on such a contention, unless the Ph.D. is alleged to be a proof of superior character as well. Yet, despite the lack of the degree (and all that this lack presumably implies) and notwithstanding their peripheral position within the discipline, the permanent non-Ph.D.'s take much the same position on professional issues as do most of their colleagues. Of course, it is possible to arrive at common conclusions by quite diverse processes of reasoning. Moreover, shared

[7] Differences on individual items were tested by chi-square test for k independent samples. The array was analyzed by both the Mann-Whitney U test and Kendall's Tau.

perceptions and values, even on intellectual issues, do not necessarily establish an equality of competence or knowledge. Our findings thus do not constitute a serious challenge to this established dogma, but neither do they provide very convincing evidence in its support.

THE NONACADEMIC POLITICAL SCIENTIST

American political science is essentially an academic as well as a learned discipline. For this reason, the problems and issues discussed in this volume—methodology, teaching versus research, publication, departmental prestige rankings, and so on—are primarily of concern to educators. Nevertheless, many political scientists pursue careers outside the world of colleges and universities. They comprise a sizable though decreasing minority (35 per cent in 1953, just under 30 per cent in 1961) of the American Political Science Association; normally have one or more representatives on the Council; frequently serve as officers of the Association; and contribute with creditable regularity to the scholarly journals. Size alone would warrant special consideration of this group in any general study of the discipline.

But there is even better cause for singling out the nonacademicians for detailed treatment. Two lines of argument suggest that on professional issues they might take a stand somewhat at variance with that of the academics. First, there may be an initial difference of values which takes one political scientist into teaching and another into, say, government service. Second, whatever the initial situation, the subsequent dissimilarity of activities and interests should produce a disparity of values and beliefs. Both of these convictions are widely held by academicians, many of whom feel that a learned discipline can be properly pursued only in an educational setting and that anyone going into some other type of endeavor is, in effect, abandoning his profession.[8]

[8] "Men who take this path [leave the academic world] are often spoken of by their colleagues as if they were literally dead—as, indeed, they are from the disciplinary point of view." Caplow and McGee, *op. cit.*, p. 150.

Readers familiar with the character of the Association's membership have perhaps been troubled by the seeming failure thus far to consider the possibilty of a divergence in attitude between these two segments of the profession. The reason for this apparent neglect is quite simple—analysis of the data on issue after issue led to the conclusion that both groups have very similar perceptions.

This finding, we must confess, took us somewhat aback. Pretest returns included several letters from nonacademics saying, in effect, that they were greatly interested in the study but that they no longer felt qualified to deal with many of the subjects encompassed by the questionnaire. However, this reaction turned out to be atypical. By and large, the nonacademic who responded to the questionnaire was as ready to take a position as was the academician —and the positions taken were closely akin.[9]

To say that the academics and the nonacademics have much in common does not, however, mean that they are identical. They differ in certain personal attributes; they also disagree on some issues. In the balance of this chapter, we shall describe some of the salient characteristics and perceptions of the nonacademics and compare these, where relevant, with those of the academic political scientists.

Personal and Occupational Characteristics

A brief sketch of the personal and occupational traits of the nonacademic will serve both to describe him and to identify the characteristics which set him apart from the academic. Since our

---

The validity of this statement would, of course, vary considerably from one discipline to the other.

[9] To be sure, there may have been a heavier incidence of responses from the nonacademicians who tended to be discipline-oriented and thus closer in attitudes to the academicians. Similarly, there may have been a lesser response from the nonacademic who was not discipline-oriented. Either or both of these biases among the respondents would have tended to minimize any possible difference in outlook between academic and nonacademic. Lastly, a very substantial percentage of those who are now nonacademics indicate in their biographical data that they have previously held positions in higher education.

description is based on systematic samples drawn from the 1953 and 1961 editions of the Association's *Directory,* we shall on occasion be able to identify possible trends.

Almost half of the nonacademic political scientists are in governmental employment. A few hold elective or appointive office; the majority are career civil servants. The remaining nonacademics are about equally divided between those associated with quasi-governmental agencies (Brookings, the several foundations, RAND, and so on) and those in business and industry.

The increased percentage of academicians in the profession (65 per cent in 1953, 70 per cent in 1961) coincided with a decrease in the number and percentage of those in the public service. College faculties expanded considerably between 1953 and 1961, and there was a concomitant marked, if not overwhelming, improvement in teaching salaries. Over the same period, civil service rolls held level or declined slightly. Although it is an article of faith among academicians that an appointment at a college or university constitutes the *summum bonum,* we really do not know whether the switch to academic employment is a true indication of the vocational preference of political scientists or is, instead, a product of the relative abundance and scarcity of jobs in these two areas.

As mentioned in the opening chapter, political science is not one of the disciplines where there has been a substantial migration of Ph.D.'s into government and industry. In 1953, about a quarter (27 per cent) of the nonacademic political scientists held earned doctorates. This percentage was essentially unchanged in 1961. Of the twenty-five respondents to the questionnaire who received doctorates in 1961 and 1962, all were employed at educational institutions. These figures make it apparent that almost none of the new Ph.D.'s is going into government or industry and suggest that very few of those already in nonacademic employment subsequently go on to take the doctorate (or that, if they do, they then tend to become academicians).

Although the academics have by far the greater incidence of doctorates, the sources of these degrees are much the same for the two categories. That is, about half of the Ph.D.'s are earned at the eleven "best" departments in the case of nonacademic and academic alike. This finding runs counter to the prevailing opinion in the profession, which, if we are not mistaken, holds that the non-academics tend to take their doctorates primarily at a few relatively unprestigious departments which cater especially to this clientele.

Although field specialization is normally associated with the academic practice of a discipline, the nonacademics identified themselves with a field about as often as did the academics. By and large, the field associations of the two groups seem to have been cut to a common pattern. Table 20 gives the field commitments for both academics and nonacademics.

TABLE 20

FIELD OF SPECIALIZATION, ACADEMICS AND NONACADEMICS

Field	Per cent Nonacademics	Per cent Academics
International relations	19.2	20.1
Comparative government	8.2	13.1
Public law	5.5	9.9
Political theory	5.5	13.9
Public administration	23.3	9.9
American government and politics	13.7	18.2
General politics and political processes	11.0	9.7

The extraordinary commitment to public administration re-flects, of course, the number of civil servants among the non-academics. Actually, the classificatory system conceals a second difference between the two occupational groups. All of the non-academics classified under "American government and politics" gave "state and local government," a subdivision of the field, as their area of specialization; less than a third of the academics classified under "American government and politics" elected this subfield identification. These differences aside, the field distributions are by no means dissimilar.

Stand on Intellectual Issues

Nonacademicians, we have said, seem to be fairly familiar with the issues currently debated in the profession. Their "index of nonfamiliarity" averaged only 5.5 "can't say" responses, as against 4.1 for the rest of the membership. The willingness to respond to a question is hardly proof of either knowledge or familiarity, but this observation applies with equal force to all political scientists.

Perhaps the greatest divergence between the academics and the nonacademics is in their stand on the three major "issue" factors. Even here, though, the differences are by no means severe, nor do they emerge on all of the factors. Thus, the nonacademics tend to be slightly more behavioralist in outlook, but the margin is so small that it can readily be attributed to chance.

A wider gap appears on the Establishment factor, although it falls just short of statistical significance ($t = 1.91$). The academics are more prone to see a powerful Establishment functioning. Assuming that the difference is not entirely casual, the most obvious explanation is that an Establishment would have less salience for the nonacademics, who, almost by definition, perform at a distance from the main body of the discipline. Furthermore, a sizable number of the nonacademics is in public administration, and we have already observed that persons in this field, for whatever reason, are lowest in their perceptions of the Establishment.

There is nothing marginal about the size of the difference ($t = 2.47$) on the factor dealing with the adequacy of the discipline. The nonacademics are distinctly the more satisfied. This manifestation of professional euphoria does not automatically prove that they lack critical acumen. For many of them, we must remember, distance may lend enchantment. Political scientists employed as practical administrators and solvers of day-to-day problems have less

occasion to become conscious of the chasm between scientific pre-
tensions and actual attainment than do those who labor to add a
widow's mite to the store of knowledge possessed by the profession.

Three statistically significant differences emerge when we examine the responses to the issues not subsumed by the three factors
in Part B of the questionnaire. In each case the disagreement is in
the direction expected. Two of these statements, Items 11 and 19,
deal respectively with nonscholarly activities and public policy matters. The nonacademics not only see less that is injurious in the
former but are more strongly convinced that political scientists do
not devote enough attention to the latter. An excellent example, we
are tempted to say, of the *apologia pro vitae suae*.

The third statement, Item 15, declares that "efforts to develop
a general theory of politics are premature." Nonacademicians are
less persuaded of this than are academicians. A plausible if not necessarily correct explanation was suggested above in discussing the
adequacy of the discipline factor. The nonacademic's job rarely
requires him to come to grips with the frustrating problems encountered in contributing to the discipline's meager stockpile of
theory. He is consequently less likely to be sensitive to the difficulty
of the task.

Both vocational categories give essentially the same weight to
the factors seen as contributing to academic advancement. On only
one item is there a difference of more than one rank, and this is
probably a chance variation. We earlier characterized the over-all
attitude of the discipline on this subject as realistic. There is certainly nothing in the background of the nonacademics, with their
considerable experience in governmental agencies, which should
make them less so. Furthermore, a goodly minority of the nonacademics have had an opportunity to observe the academic world
from within.[10]

Nonacademics tend to be somewhat less satisfied with political
science as a career than are the academics. When asked whether,
if free to start over, they would still choose political science as a
career, 67.1 per cent of the former and 77.8 per cent of the latter

[10] Thirty-seven per cent in 1953 and 48 per cent in 1961 had taught
in colleges or universities.

said definitely or probably yes. These differences fall short of statistical significance. Elbridge Sibley asked a similar question of academic and nonacademic sociologists who hold Ph.D.'s. Although the wording of the two queries and the different sets of answer options offered to respondents suggest caution in comparing the results, it does seem that political scientists with doctorates are substantially more satisfied with their choice of career than are their counterparts in sociology. In the next chapter we shall treat this and other aspects of career satisfaction at greater length.

Thus, in each of the areas examined, the evidence of fundamental agreement between academics and nonacademics is impressive. Part of this may be attributed, as noted at the outset of this discussion, to a possible overrepresentation of discipline-oriented nonacademics in the respondents to our questionnaire. Nevertheless, we would doubt that this is a sufficient explanation for the similarities of attitudes observed. In any case, it seems clear that the nonacademic political scientist is at most a species in the larger genus rather than, as many have thought, a breed apart.

-12-
Career Satisfaction

There are many standards by which a discipline can be judged. We might assess, for example, its contributions to human knowledge, its prestige and standing among the other sciences, or the material rewards enjoyed by its practitioners. Another yardstick would be the influence it exerts on public policy and the part it plays in molding public opinion. Or, looking inward, we might ask whether the members of that discipline are satisfied with their chosen careers. Not all of these matters lend themselves to ready measurement; even if they did, the results might vary with the criterion applied. From the viewpoint of the practitioners themselves, however, the last standard mentioned is perhaps the ultimate one—"For what is a man profited, if he shall gain the whole world, and lose his own soul?" Political scientists are all too effectively protected against the hazard of gaining the world, but how well have their collective souls been attended? That is the question to which this chapter is devoted, and there could hardly be a more fitting subject with which to conclude the study of a learned discipline.

We shall seek three objectives in the following pages: first, to describe the extent to which political scientists are happy with their chosen careers; next, to account for the dissatisfaction which does exist; finally, to assay the implications for the profession of the present level of satisfaction and dissatisfaction among its membership.

CAREER SATISFACTION

To measure career satisfaction, we employed Section D-1 of the questionnaire: "If you were able to start over and pick your profession again, would you still choose a career in political science?" Respondents had a choice of five options: "definitely yes," "probably yes," "can't say," "probably not," and "definitely not." Table 21 summarizes their answers.

TABLE 21

WILLINGNESS TO CHOOSE POLITICAL SCIENCE AGAIN

Respondents	Def. yes	Prob. yes	Can't say*	Prob. not	Def. not	Total
Number	162	161	40	56	6	425 †
Percentage	38.1	37.9	9.4	13.2	1.4	100.0

* "Can't says" include those not answering the question.

† To avoid confusion which may otherwise result because of the variables used in the subsequent analysis, six cases for whom we have no information on type of employment have been excluded from this table.

Two aspects of Table 21 are particularly noteworthy. A vast majority would give political science another try. The "definitely yes" and "probably yes" choices, almost equal in size, together account for some three-quarters (76 per cent) of the total. Furthermore, not all of the remaining answers are negative, since nearly 10 per cent of the respondents were not willing to come down one way or another. Depending on the base selected, then, either 24 per cent are not prepared to say they would do it again or 15 per cent are prepared to concede that they would not. Equally striking is the small size of the group who gave a "definitely not" reply. Barely one political scientist in a hundred, it would seem, is so acutely dissatisfied that he is ready to elect this answer.[1]

THE BASES FOR CAREER DISSATISFACTION

The conclusions to be drawn from the finding that three (or should we say *only* three?) out of four political scientists are satisfied with their profession depend in part on the reasons which lead a minority to say that they would *not* again choose the same career path. These reasons might range from frustrated personal ambitions to discontent with the discipline itself. Though the instrument used to measure career satisfaction does not permit as precise an answer as we might wish, the data do allow us to test the validity of various explanations. The more plausible of these will be stated as hypotheses, and the relevant evidence will then be examined. (Thus far, we have tried to avoid formalistic treatment of our findings. The nature of the data here, however, seems to mandate a recourse to the "hypothesis-data-conclusion" format.)

Hypothesis 1

Career satisfaction is related to type of employment, possession of a Ph.D., and both of these.

[1] In fact, it is possible to argue that the six "definitely not" responses should be reduced to only four. One person checking "definitely not" pointed out that, although a member of the American Political Science Association, he is really an economist. Another, a retired Army officer, commented that he very much enjoys being a political scientist but that he was taking this option because his heart still belongs to the military. It makes no practical difference whether we count six or four "definitely nots." For analytical purposes, it is obviously best to take the answer given by each respondent at face value.

As pointed out in previous chapters, nonacademic political scientists and academic political scientists who lack doctorates can be viewed as out-groups within the discipline. Those who share one or both of these characteristics might therefore be expected to display somewhat less satisfaction with political science than the dominant in-group, the academic Ph.D.'s. Table 22 presents the data necessary to test this expectation.

TABLE 22

CAREER SATISFACTION OF CERTAIN SUBGROUPS IN STUDY
(IN PERCENTAGES)

	Responses					
	Def. yes	Prob. yes	Can't say*	Prob. not	Def. not	Total
All respondents (N = 425)†	38.1	37.9	9.4	13.2	1.4	100.0
All academics (N = 352)	39.2	38.6	8.2	12.8	1.1	99.9
Ph.D.'s (N = 302)	40.7	38.1	7.6	12.9	.7	100.0
Non-Ph.D.'s (N = 50)	30.0	42.0	12.0	12.0	4.0	100.0
Nonacademics (N = 73)	32.9	34.2	15.1	15.1	2.7	100.0
Ph.D.'s (N = 26)	34.6	38.5	15.4	7.7	3.8	100.0
Non-Ph.D.'s (N = 47)	31.9	31.9	14.9	19.1	2.1	99.9

* "Can't says" include those not answering the question.
† The six respondents for whom type of employment is unknown were excluded, thus reducing the sample size to 425.

Career satisfaction, it seems clear, is relatively independent either of type of employment or of possession of a doctorate. The "definitely yes" column, for example, reveals that the academic Ph.D.'s are the most satisfied group and the academic non-Ph.D.'s the least. This finding is in line with expectation, but the 10.7 per cent difference carries relatively little weight for a subsample of this size.

When the "definitely yes" and "probably yes" answers are combined, it is the nonacademic non-Ph.D.'s who emerge as the least satisfied, again in line with expectation. Still, almost two-thirds of those lacking both doctorates and academic posts express satisfaction with political science; hardly more than one in five (21.2 per cent) declare that they would turn elsewhere next time. All in all, neither type of employment nor the possession of a doctorate, singly or in combination, offers much in the way of an answer to the question, *"Who* is dissatisfied?" let alone, *"Why* is he dissatisfied?"

Hypothesis 2

Career dissatisfaction on the part of academic Ph.D.'s is related to the prestige of the departments at which they are employed.

A majority of American political scientists are academic Ph.D.'s. For a study concerned with political science as a learned discipline, they comprise not only the largest, but in many respects the most important, group of the profession. Hypotheses 2, 3, 4, and 5 are thus specifically intended to explore dissatisfaction among this group.

American political science departments fall into a fairly well-defined and generally recognized hierarchy. There is a profound difference in status between the "best" dozen or so graduate departments, on the one hand, and the remaining departments, graduate and undergraduate, on the other. This formulation does not deny the existence of subclasses in each of these two basic categories nor of important status gradations among the undergraduate departments. All in all, however, a full professorship at one of the prestigious graduate departments constitutes the capstone of a successful career.

Given this situation, it is reasonable to predict that men with appointments at prestigious departments will be more satisfied than those at less distinguished institutions. Whatever the plausibility of the expectation, the data do it violence. There is virtually no correlation between the prestige of departmental affiliation and willingness or reluctance to serve out the next reincarnation as a political scientist.

Hypothesis 3

Career dissatisfaction among academic Ph.D.'s is related to the frustration of career aspirations as defined by appointments commensurate with prestige of doctorate.

The failure to confirm Hypothesis 2 led us to reconsider and then to restate the relationship. The original formulation assumed that an objective mark of achievement (type of appointment) should be reflected in a corresponding sense of satisfaction. But the latter is a state of mind and subject to all the vagaries thereof. Might not a *feeling* of achievement depend more on fulfilling the aspirations one has set for himself than on any objective measure of success? Surely, what might be a most rewarding career for someone with modest goals might be near complete frustration for a more ambitious person. By treating career satisfaction primarily as a function of accomplishment, unrelated to aspiration, we may have improperly posited and, accordingly, failed to uncover an explanation for dissatisfaction.

The difficulty with the hypothesis as reformulated is that we have no direct evidence of the respondents' aspirations. For want of anything better, we utilized an *ad hoc* measure—doctoral origins. School of Ph.D., we have seen, is widely believed to be an important element in career advancement. We therefore postulated a relationship between aspirations and doctoral origins, to wit: that persons coming from prestigious departments would have loftier ambitions than those with degrees from more humble sources. If this assumption were valid, it should follow that political scientists holding appointments in departments as prestigious as the ones at which they took their doctorates would be more satisfied than political scientists employed at departments lower in the hierarchy than those at which they earned their degrees and vice versa. To test Hypothesis 3 as thus rendered operational, Table 23 was constructed.

TABLE 23

CAREER SATISFACTION BY SOURCE OF DOCTORATE AND
SCHOOL OF EMPLOYMENT
(IN PERCENTAGES)*

| | Source of Ph.D. | | |
| | Top 11 departments ($N = 137$) | 22 "other" rated departments† ($N = 113$) | All departments not rated ($N = 19$) |
Employed at			
Top 11 graduate departments ($N = 34$)	88.0	‡	‡
22 "other" rated graduate departments ($N = 56$)	87.1	77.2	‡
All departments not rated ($N = 216$)	82.7	87.1	91.3

* "Can't says" not used in computing percentages.
† Rated schools are those included on Section C-7 of questionnaire.
‡ Fewer than ten cases.

The data here are probably easier to grasp than the structure of the table, and a word or two of explanation may facilitate its use. All academic Ph.D.'s who gave "definitely yes" or "probably yes" answers to Item D-1 were classified as satisfied; those who checked the "definitely not" or "probably not" boxes, as dissatisfied. The percentage of satisfied persons was then calculated for each of the nine cells shown.

Careful attention to the contents of Table 23 can lead to only one conclusion—the data lend meager support, at the very most, to

Hypothesis 3. This does not mean that career satisfaction may not be related to career aspirations. However, it certainly does demonstrate that this relationship, if it exists, is not reflected in our assumption about the respective aspirations of those with high- and low-prestige doctorates. Whether the defect is in the hypothesis, in the assumption, or in both cannot be determined on the basis of the evidence presently available.

Hypothesis 4

Career dissatisfaction is related to failure to fulfill aspirations as defined in terms of intrainstitutional promotion.

There is another way in which the hypothesized relationship between satisfaction and aspirations might be tested, although this alternative bears less on political scientists as professionals than as professors. If we assume that political scientists qua academic men aspire to recognition by their own institutions in the form of reasonably timely promotions, then the younger persons at any given level should be more satisfied than their elders holding the same grade. This would not necessarily apply to full professors, because they have reached the top of the ladder (some of them many years ago) and would presumably have nothing more to aspire to at their own institutions.

To test this variant of the satisfaction-aspiration theory, therefore, only academic Ph.D.'s below full professor were studied. Age categories developed for another purpose[2] were employed to separate instructors, assistant professors, and associate professors into two groups—those considered to be old for the rank held and those who were younger. Table 24 shows the results.

The reader who has persevered through the demise of three preceding hypotheses is finally rewarded. For the first time in our quest for possible causes of career dissatisfaction, sizable and statis-

[2] Albert Somit and Joseph Tanenhaus, "Trends in American Political Science: Some Analytical Notes," *American Political Science Review*, LVII, No. 4 (1963), 933–947.

tically significant differences appear. Persons relatively old for their
rank tend to be considerably less satisfied with the profession than
are their younger equals. Even though only three in ten of this
older group admit to career dissatisfaction, the figures are more

TABLE 24

CAREER SATISFACTION:
YOUNGER AND OLDER PH.D.'S HOLDING RANKS BELOW
FULL PROFESSOR*

	Younger		Older	
	Number	Per cent	Number	Per cent
Satisfied ("definitely" and "probably yes")	97	93.3	45	70.3
Dissatisfied ("definitely" and "probably not")	7	6.7	19	29.7
Total	104	100.0	64	100.0

* "Can't says" were not used in computing these percentages.

telling than they initially seem. Individuals slow to be promoted
constitute only 23 per cent of the academic Ph.D.'s, but they supply
almost half (47 per cent) of the dissatisfied responses. On the other
hand, the political scientists relatively young for their rank make
up 37 per cent of the academic doctorates, but only 17 per cent of
them indicate that, given another chance, they would not choose
political science again.

However useful Hypothesis 4 may be in accounting for the
dissatisfaction of some persons with unfulfilled aspirations, it cannot possibly explain the discontent expressed by those whose intrainstitutional recognition is fully commensurate with even the loftiest
of expectations. In the eternal quest for happiness, it appears, the
race is not always to the swift.

Hypothesis 5

Career dissatisfaction is related to low esteem for political science as a learned discipline.

As noted in Chapter 3, factor analysis showed that a substantial measure of the variance in the responses to the twenty-six issue statements could be accounted for by a dimension we termed "adequacy of the profession." Is it possible that some political scientists are dissatisfied with their profession not because of unfulfilled aspirations (as defined), but because they feel that political science lacks the theory and techniques needed to deal competently with its subject matter? This hypothesis can be tested by comparing the adequacy-factor scores for the persons who expressed career satisfaction with those of the persons who did not. The difference turns out to be statistically significant ($t = 2.35$).

Additional support for the validity of Hypothesis 5 emerges when we compare the responses of the satisfied and dissatisfied respondents to the twenty-three issue statements not subsumed by the adequacy factor. T tests disclose that the statements on which they differ most are:

Item   5. By and large, the preparation of a doctoral dissertation in political science is not an intellectually satisfying experience.
Item 11. The involvement of political scientists in non-scholarly activities has tended to impede the development of the discipline.
Item 20. Political science has generally competed rather successfully with the other social sciences in areas of common interest and study.

The differences on the first two are significant at the .05 level of confidence; that on the third just falls short of it ($t = 1.75$).

Of the five hypotheses advanced, two (4 and 5) were confirmed. But what does this really mean? After all, statistical significance is a function of sample size. The larger the number of cases, the greater the likelihood that a relationship of a given magnitude will prove significant. The subsample of academic Ph.D.'s contains enough cases so that relationships which do not account for much of the variance in career satisfaction can still be statistically significant. Furthermore, the two confirmed hypotheses may overlap to a considerable extent. Low esteem for the discipline may be largely the result of frustrated personal ambitions. If so, the two hypotheses taken together would not account for much more career dissatisfaction than either of them alone.

Consequently, the kinds of questions which still remained to be answered were: How much of the dissatisfaction expressed can be attributed to unfulfilled aspirations? How much to a low esteem for the discipline? How much to stand on behavioralism, perception of the Establishment, and other variables? Finally, how much remains unexplained either because the relevant hypotheses have escaped us or because we lack, in whole or in part, the data needed to test those which have occurred? To deal with these questions we employed a more powerful statistic—multiple correlation and regression analysis.

The answers provided by this technique are that (1) unfulfilled aspirations (Hypothesis 4) and low esteem for the discipline (Hypothesis 5) are completely independent of one another as predictors of career dissatisfaction; (2) unfulfilled aspirations (Hypothesis 4) account for less career dissatisfaction than does low esteem for the discipline (Hypothesis 5); (3) neither unfulfilled aspirations nor low esteem for political science is responsible for enough variance in satisfaction-dissatisfaction to be considered a major explanation;[3] (4) the behavioralism and Establishment factors are not useful predictors of career satisfaction; and (5) the issue items not subsumed by any of the factors or Hypothesis 5 do not add anything worth mentioning. The most important inference to be drawn from this analysis, then, is a reassuring one: whatever the cause of dis-

---

[3] Together they account for less than 10 per cent of the variance. The computer programs used for this analysis were the BIMD 06 and the BIMD 09.

satisfaction among our academic Ph.D.'s, they do not seem readily attributable to unhappiness with political science as a learned discipline.

IMPLICATIONS FOR THE DISCIPLINE

We have already described the level of satisfaction expressed by the respondents. Some 76 per cent said they would probably or definitely choose a career in political science again; 15 per cent said that they probably or definitely would not; and the remainder, in effect, were noncommittal. Do these findings reflect a healthy ratio of satisfaction to dissatisfaction, or are they cause for serious concern? Without comparable data for an earlier period or for other learned disciplines, this would normally be about as easy to resolve as, "How high is up?"

Fortunately, Elbridge Sibley, in his recent study of American sociologists, included a question on career satisfaction similar enough to that used in our own inquiry to permit the addition of another dimension to this analysis. Because the questions employed in the two surveys are similar rather than identical, their exact wording should be noted. Sibley phrased his free-response query as follows: "If you were to begin your *graduate education* over again, would you seek a Ph.D. degree in sociology? If not, why, and what would be your alternative choice?" Our corresponding item was: "If you were able to start over and pick your profession again, would you still choose a career in political science?" The options offered were the five listed above. In Table 25 we have attempted to present the data from both studies in a form suitable for comparison.

Keeping in mind the differences both in the wording of the two questions and in the answer options offered, we find that several observations are in order. For one thing, the difference in dissatisfaction levels between all Ph.D.'s in political science (22 per cent) and in sociology (28 per cent) is not great. Nevertheless, for samples as large as these, it is not negligible. For another thing, the academic Ph.D.'s are not the principal source of the variation. In fact, the two percentage points separating sociologists and political scientists can be readily dismissed as a chance divergence. The non-academic Ph.D.'s, however, differ to a degree which is fairly impressive, despite the small size of the political science sample.

Why is it that nonacademic political scientists seem to be happier than their counterparts in sociology? A number of ideas come to mind, but, given the available data (and Sibley's are more relevant than ours), it would be foolhardy even to speculate about them at this time.[4] The reasons for the relatively greater satisfaction

TABLE 25

COMPARATIVE CAREER DISSATISFACTION: POLITICAL
SCIENCE AND SOCIOLOGY*

	Percentages of Ph.D.'s not sure they would again choose	
	Career in political science	Ph.D. in sociology
All Ph.D.'s	22 $(N = 328)$	28 $(N = 401)$
Academic Ph.D.'s	21 $(N = 302)$	23 $(N > 100)$
Nonacademic Ph.D.'s	27 $(N = \ 26)$	44 $(N > 100)$

* Sociology data from Sibley, *op. cit.*, p. 160, Table 53.

among these political scientists vis-a-vis the sociologists must be left for future inquiry.

The almost identical levels of dissatisfaction manifested by academic political scientists and sociologists raise the interesting

[4] Is it the relative suitability of the professional training received for the kind of work they are called upon to do? Or is it that the persons with whom the sociologist is competing make his training seem relatively inadequate, whereas this is less true for the political scientist? Can it be that the jobs political scientists tend to get are intrinsically more interesting or financially more rewarding than those which go to sociologists? Or do the jobs which sociologists obtain fall shorter of their aspirations than those obtained by political scientists do of theirs?

possibility that the wellsprings of discontent are to be found in college and university life rather than in any particular learned discipline. Further plausibility is lent to this conjecture by our failure to relate career satisfaction strongly to attitudes on issues of concern to the discipline. Whether the basic causes of dissatisfaction are inherent in academia itself will not be known, however, until we have adequate general investigations of faculty morale. These, unfortunately, are still at exploratory stages.[5] And perhaps even after all the studies are done and all the evidence is in, we may have to concede that the answer we seek still remains hidden in the "ancient and unexplored caverns of the human spirit."[6]

[5] See John E. Stecklein and Robert L. Lathrop, *Faculty Attraction and Retention: Factors Affecting Faculty Mobility at the University of Minnesota* (Minneapolis: Bureau of Institutional Research, University of Minnesota, 1960); John Dale Russell, "Faculty Satisfactions and Dissatisfactions," *The Journal of Experimental Education,* XXXI, No. 2 (1962), 135–139; Joseph Tanenhaus, Sidney X. Roth, and Robert H. Lilienfeld, "Faculty Satisfactions and Dissatisfactions: A Methodological Study of Part II of the Russell Questionnaire," in L. Joseph Lins, ed., *The Role of Institutional Research in Planning* (Madison: Office of Institutional Studies, University of Wisconsin, 1963), pp. 93–120; Robert L. Lathrop, "Assessment of Faculty Satisfactions and Dissatisfactions Through Mobility Studies," *ibid.,* pp. 121–126.

[6] Lawrence S. Kubie, "Some Unsolved Problems of the Scientific Career," in Barber and Hirsch, *op. cit.,* p. 203.

Postface

With some optimism, this book is subtitled "A Profile of a Discipline." As we sought to make clear in our opening pages and in the ensuing chapters, the data at hand permit only a profile rather than a full-length portrait. Having stressed the need for additional information, we feel a certain responsibility to indicate the directions which further inquiry might take. On the other hand, we have in this volume sought to avoid programmatic recommendations, seeing our role as that of *rapporteurs* and analysts rather than reformers or critics. An action agenda would thus be out of keeping, if not actually incongruous, with this approach.

Faced with these conflicting imperatives, we adopted a compromise solution. In the interests of textual purity, no research proposals are presented in the main body of the book. Those interested in this subject will, however, find in Appendix C a statement of the areas and topics to which, in our opinion, students of American political science might profitably turn their attention.

-A-
Methodological Note

This note is intended primarily for those interested in the methodology employed in the compilation and analysis of the data for this study. We shall deal here with aspects of the subject considered too technical or esoteric for treatment in the body of the volume. The sequence of discussion will be (1) sampling methods and (2) types of descriptive and inferential statistics utilized.

SAMPLING METHODS

The critical question for this type of study is whether the sample responses are truly representative of the universe from which the sample was drawn.

Representativeness

Since we sought to generalize about American political science (and political scientists) on the basis of mailed questionnaire responses, it was not enough merely to draw a systematic sample of the American Political Science Association's membership. There was, in addition, the need to exorcise that perennial evil spirit of mailed surveys—the possibility that the responses, however gratifying in size, were representative neither of the sample nor of the universe under study. Toward this end, two separate techniques were employed.

We placed major reliance on the following technique. Data were compiled from the 1961 *Directory* for each of the 832 persons to whom questionnaires were eventually sent. These data, which included year of birth, source and date of degree(s), employment, rank, and so on, were then coded and punched on Hollerith cards. Part A, the background section of the questionnaire, provided enough comparable data from each respondent so that, once this information had been punched on another set of cards, the two could be collated by machine. By this device we were able to match the two cards for 425 of the 431 persons returning usable questionnaires and to compare the *Directory* data cards for respondents and nonrespondents on the several parameters available.[1]

The comparisons disclosed only a single bias in our returns—academic members of the Association are somewhat overrepresented and nonacademic members somewhat underrepresented. Slightly better than 80 per cent of the replies came from academics, whereas this group constitutes just a bit better than 70 per cent of the profession's membership. This skewing probably stems from four sources. The names of political scientists in high public office were deleted from the sample; information on the current addresses of nonacademics turned out to be comparatively less reliable; some

[1] As we assumed that the respondents would prefer anonymity, the questionnaires were not numbered or otherwise coded. Several dozen persons, nevertheless, deliberately identified themselves.

nonacademics do not really consider themselves professional political scientists; and, since the questionnaire is primarily oriented toward matters of academic concern, some nonacademics felt that they had been too long out of touch to venture opinions on the topics covered by the questionnaire.

Everything considered, we do not think that this bias seriously affects the representative nature of the responses. In fact, given our focus on political science as a learned *and* academic discipline, we might say that this is perhaps the best of all possible biases.

The second method used to test representativeness, although quite conventional, is of only minor importance. Partial analyses were made of the first 120 questionnaires returned; the results were compared with similar analyses for the next 244 replies and then with the remaining completed questionnaires. All three waves were extremely stable for each area tested—the twenty-six issue statements in Part B, the considerations bearing on ability to get offers from other schools (C-6), and the over-all quality of doctoral programs (C-7). The similarity of the three subsamples further indicated that the responses mirrored the larger universe from which the total sample was drawn.

Sampling Techniques

Two separate samples were drawn, one for the pretest and another for the study proper. Since the latter was actually developed first, we will begin with it and then take up the manner in which the pretest sample was later chosen.

Every fifth name was selected from the 1961 *Directory* of the American Political Science Association and a directory data sheet prepared from the accompanying biographical sketch.[2] Each person for whom there were no data about degrees was replaced by the first name immediately following which gave this information. The "News and Notes" sections of the *American Political Science Re-*

[2] This sketch is, of course, based on information supplied by the member himself.

view from March, 1960, to December, 1962, were used to update mailing addresses, employment, and academic rank.

After the data sheets had been updated, the following classes were removed from the sample: known deceased, full-time students, persons abroad for academic year 1963–1964, and such high public officials as United States senators, members of the president's cabinet, and presidential administrative assistants. The deletion of full-time students we now believe, from the wisdom of hindsight, to have been a mistake. On the other hand, the soundness of the decision to remove high public officials was confirmed by a letter from an eminent senator who somehow slipped through the screening procedures. He wrote:

> I would like to take the time to fill out your questionnaire, but the truth is I am swamped with legislative work and unable to take on any additional tasks at this time.
>
> Very frankly, students of political science send me so many questionnaires that were I to comply with their requests, I would have no time to do my work. As a Senator, moreover, I had thought that most political scientists recognize by now the questionable validity of studies conducted in this manner. I could, as most do, give it to one of my assistants to fill out, but I don't think you would appreciate this and certainly it would not be very "scientific."

After the removal of the groups indicated, 832 names remained. These 832 political scientists constituted the study sample. A copy of the revised questionnaire, together with a personally addressed robotyped letter explaining the purpose of the study, was mailed to each on March 27, 1963.

Not until the study sample was drawn were the pretest respondents selected. The reason, of course, was to make sure that the former did not include anyone earmarked for the latter.

To choose the pretest group, we took the name of the person at the top of every fourth column of the 1961 *Directory*. Once again, the biographical sketches were updated by using "News and Notes." From this roster of 141 names, we deleted the same categories eliminated from the study sample as well as those who fell among the 832 chosen for the study sample. Again, at least one person slipped through the screening procedures, for one respondent wrote that he had received both questionnaires.

From the more than one hundred remaining names, we constructed a stratified sample of seventy-two persons. Stratification was undertaken to ensure that the pretest group included political scientists with and without doctorates, those holding nonacademic as well as academic posts, a wide range of age groups, field representation, and a cross section of persons from institutions of varying sizes, types, and geographic locations. A copy of the printed pretest questionnaire, together with a personally addressed robotyped covering letter, went to each of the pretest sample members on February 27, 1963. There was nothing in either the letter or the questionnaire to indicate that this was a pretest rather than the actual survey itself.

Sample Response

The time schedule under which we were working required that the revised questionnaire go to the printer by no later than March 20. Accordingly, only the pretest responses received prior to this date could be used in revising the questionnaire. Thirty-nine came back within this time; another fourteen were returned too late to be helpful. Of the thirty-nine, more than two-thirds contained written comments, some quite extensive. While these comments did not produce any major structural changes, they did persuade us to make a substantial number of revisions in the questionnaire. We have frequently alluded to the value of the pretest responses in preceding chapters. In order that the reader may have an accurate picture of the character of these changes, both questionnaires are included in Appendix B.

Twenty-five of the 832 questionnaires were eventually returned as undeliverable. By May 1, 1963, the date on which final coding began, we had received responses from 454 of the 807 individuals to whom questionnaires were presumably delivered. An additional twenty questionnaires came in after May 1, but these could not be included in the analysis.

Of the 454 persons who responded before the cutoff date, 431 sent back usable questionnaires. The two dozen losses resulted from failure to complete essential sections of the instrument or refusals to participate, generally because the recipient had been away from political science for a long time or else did not regard himself as a member of the discipline. Three letters came from widows or the executors of estates, despite our efforts to avoid such mishaps. As with the pretest, a substantial number of the respondents appended comments. We have acknowledged the value of these at appropriate places in the text.

STATISTICAL TECHNIQUES

A variety of descriptive and inferential statistics was used in the course of this study. Although we tried hard not to overburden the reader whose interests in methodology are slender, we also attempted, in text and chapter notes, to inform the technician of the statistical bases for the inferences drawn from the data. It is, however, appropriate to offer some additional comments in this appendix.

Statistics Used to Analyze the Issues

We have assumed that the responses to the twenty-six issue statements satisfy the requirements of interval measurement. That is, we assigned the following weights to each category of response: "strongly agree," five; "generally agree," four; "can't say," three; "generally disagree," two; and "definitely disagree," one. This assumption treats "can't say" responses as the mid-point on a five-point scale, the gradations of which reflect equal intervals of intensity.

We are aware of the difficulty in demonstrating that Likert-type scale responses are ordinal, let alone interval. But, as S. S.

Stevens points out, one can sometimes defend on pragmatic grounds the use of statistics whose models postulate a level of measurement one has not clearly met.[3] In our opinion—and it must to a degree be intuitive—the powerful kinds of multivariate analysis made possible by regarding these responses as falling on interval scales fully justify whatever error may have thereby been introduced.

The technique relied on most heavily in working with the twenty-six issue statements was factor analysis, although greater use was made of a variety of parametric statistics in probing these data than may be evident from the text. The major purpose for utilizing factor analysis was not to test hypotheses but to describe responses involving many variables in terms of a small number of basic components which could then be treated as substitutes for the variables they subsumed.

After some initial misgivings we decided that the most appropriate type of factoring for these statements would be an orthogonal simple-structure solution employing Kaiser's varimax method, using SMC's rather than unities as the estimates of communality and rotating a number of factors equal to the number of eigenvalues greater than zero. This is perhaps an oversimplified statement, but we prefer to avoid technical jargon wherever possible. The computer program utilized was the BIMD 17, case option number 3. Since intuitive elements necessarily play a part in interpreting a factor analysis, we have reproduced immediately below the rotated matrix for the five largest factors, together with the cumulative proportion of the variance accounted for by them.

Factors 3 and 4 were not used in this study, primarily because they proved highly unstable on many of the factor analyses we ran on subgroups of the discipline. Instead, we discussed the individual statements not subsumed by Factors 1 (behavioralism), 2 (adequacy of the discipline), and 5 (Establishment) whenever they seemed to illuminate the perceptions of sample subgroups.

The argument in the text frequently required factor scores for each respondent on each of the three key factors. These individual

[3] S. S. Stevens, "On the Theory of Scales of Measurement," in Arthur Danto and Sidney Morgenbesser, eds., *Philosophy of Science* (Cleveland and New York: Meridian Books, 1960), pp. 145–146.

TABLE 26

ROTATED FACTOR MATRIX

			Factor		
Issue	1	2	3	4	5
1	.22468	.30285	.13223	.06895	.09474
2	—.01710	.21954	.43139	.08008	.03413
3	.08213	.53788	.10410	.05302	—.06088
4	.34993	.16919	.08067	.13791	.21308
5	.05035	.19794	—.04363	.16519	.07059
6	.69892	—.05890	—.08724	.19682	.17800
7	—.04529	.61878	.03391	.04413	.04031
8	—.12246	.62002	.03570	—.08058	.02808
9	.43265	.03104	.01264	.09557	.10203
10	—.42170	.00892	.11743	—.02870	—.11511
11	.01261	.31344	—.03448	—.28424	.12344
12	.04865	.14432	.36778	—.01130	—.02687
13	.15355	.03219	.04561	.48729	.03718
14	—.13374	—.10090	.51825	—.03019	—.17904
15	.28181	—.01801	.07141	.03398	—.02600
16	.13377	.01196	—.07052	.06216	.54337
17	—.02478	.04065	.13004	—.05383	.04820
18	.20240	.09366	—.04117	.32119	.20905
19	.08997	.00492	—.03818	.47260	.02781
20	.24077	—.22042	—.09323	—.12839	—.12365
21	—.06051	.10723	—.00654	.03499	.03699
22	.75727	—.00703	—.05758	.11996	.11247
23	.77236	—.01201	—.05741	.06134	.07082
24	—.05725	.02203	.44653	—.01997	.02061
25	.22001	—.01069	.06296	.08138	.15973
26	.12444	.02979	—.03159	—.01604	.62004
Cumulative proportion of variance	.38358	.59501	.69400	.77141	.84088

factor scores were computed by the following procedure. For each statement with a rotated matrix loading of at least .400 on a designated factor, the actual magnitude of the loading was multiplied by the weight assigned to that response. This weight was adjusted for direction when necessary. The resulting products for the several statements were then summed to give each respondent a score for each factor. There were two reasons for setting a loading of .400 as the minimum for including a statement in the computation of factor scores. First, the relationship is highly significant at this level (greater than three standard deviations), and, second, no statement had a loading that high on more than one factor.

Statistics Used in Analyzing Parts of the Questionnaire

Data for Parts C-5, C-6, and C-7 of the questionnaire, dealing respectively with journals, departmental prestige, and the considerations leading to outside job offers, were treated as no more than ordinal. On several occasions indexes requiring a weighting of responses had to be constructed, but the index scores were not considered interval measures and none of the so-called parametric statistics was used in analyzing them.

Although we experimented with numerous methods of constructing indexes, the final decision was to employ a uniform technique for ordering these particular data. This involved weighting "great" and "excellent" responses as three; "some" or "good" as two; and "very little" or "fair" as one. The response weights were added together and then divided by the number of respondents who selected one of the weighted options *plus* those who answered "not at all," "poor," or "none." "Can't say" responses and failures to answer were completely excluded in the computation of indexes. The resulting scores were treated as constituting no more than ordinal scales.

Tests of Significance

Variations in answer patterns to two or more items, as well as variations among sample groups, represent real differences for the respondents involved. But can one legitimately generalize about the attitudes and perceptions of the entire discipline from these responses? Yes, if two requirements are satisfied. First, the respondents must constitute a random sample of the universe from which they were drawn; we have already discussed why we believe that the respondents in this study are representative of political scientists as a whole. Second, there must be some method for determining whether the answers obtained reflect real differences in the universe of political scientists or whether they could more properly be attributed to sampling error.

Many tests are available for determining the likelihood that similarities or dissimilarities between two or more random samples are the result of sampling error. In deciding which to use in a given situation, we were guided by three criteria: the test should be appropriate to the need; the test should be generally known and accepted; and, to the extent consonant with the preceding requirements, the number of tests employed should be as small as possible. Accordingly, we utilized chi-square tests when working with nominal data and the Kruskal-Wallis one-way analysis of variance, the Mann-Whitney U, Kendall's tau, and Kendall's coefficient of concordance when the data were regarded as ordinal. Both t and F tests were used in dealing with the twenty-six issue statements. The level of confidence set throughout this study has been .05 (two-tailed) unless there is specific indication to the contrary. Since the tests were used in roughly comparable situations, we have taken pains to identify each test by name the first few times. Thereafter they are named only where there is some danger of confusion as to which is being applied.

In preparing the tables in this volume, we have usually indicated the probable significance of a relationship with the convention "P (Ho)" rather than simply "P." Although it may seem an unnecessary touch of formalism, this device was adopted because not all of the tests used were designed to measure the same kind of relationship. "Ho," by specifically calling attention to the null hypothesis, acts as a warning flag. This is particularly important when the relationship under examination is one of similarity rather than of difference. If the null hypothesis is kept clearly in mind, the risk of misreading these tests is greatly diminished.

None of the foregoing, we hasten to add, is intended to suggest that we accepted the results of significance tests at face value. After all, they are at best highly arbitrary, if impersonal, devices for ascertaining the likelihood that a given relationship resulted from sampling variation. There is always some danger that a test of significance might lead to the rejection of real differences or the acceptance of spurious ones. Furthermore, as noted repeatedly in the text, not only is statistical significance a function of sample size, but a statistically significant relationship may also account for very little of the variance under scrutiny. We have therefore treated significance tests as highly suggestive, but no more. In our judgment, plausibility and the relationships among hypotheses, together with a certain aesthetic sense, must be used in conjunction with these techniques in determining the inferences to be drawn from data similar to those on which this study is based.

-B-1-
Pretest Questionnaire

QUESTIONNAIRE ON THE STATE OF
AMERICAN POLITICAL SCIENCE[1]

A. Background Data
    1. Year of birth:
    2. Year of degree(s) and name of school(s) awarding degree:

Degree	Year of degree	School
B.A., B.S., etc.		
M.A., M.S., etc.		
Ph.D.		
other		

---

[1] The questionnaire has been edited slightly to conform with the style of the text.

3. If you had to identify yourself with a single field in political science, which one would it be?

B. The following observations have been made in the past few years in the literature dealing with the state of the discipline. On the whole, how do you feel about each of them? (Check "agree strongly," "agree," "disagree," "disagree strongly," or "can't say.")

1. Much that passes for scholarship in political science is superficial or trivial.

2. Political scientists in the United States are unhappy about the current state of their discipline.

3. Political science cannot be said to have any generally agreed upon body of methods and techniques.

4. Much research in political science is undertaken simply because the projects lend themselves to research by a fashionable tool or because financial support can readily be secured.

5. By and large, the preparation of a doctoral dissertation in political science is not an intellectually satisfying experience.

6. The American Political Science Association is democratically controlled and responsive to the wishes of its members.

7. Communication among political scientists is seriously hindered by the inadequacy of their basic concepts.

8. Political scientists tend to be unsophisticated about the nature of scientific investigation.

9. Efforts to formulate, refine, and clarify concepts and to obtain agreements on labels to be attached to concepts result in little more than hairsplitting and jargon.

10. The articles currently being published in the *American Political Science Review* are of a generally better quality than those published before World War II.

11. The involvement of political scientists in nonscholarly activities has impeded the development of the discipline.

12. A substantial part of the intellectual conflict in American political science is rooted in issues that are methodological in character.

13. Doctoral programs in political science stress research training at the cost of preparing effective undergraduate teachers.

14. The mood of contemporary American political science is one of stock-taking and self-criticism.

15. Given the present state of political science, efforts to develop a general theory of politics are premature.

16. American political science has developed an Establishment which largely determines the character and standards of the discipline.

17. If we have to learn calculus and probability theory, we might as well give up political science and take up physics.

18. A high proportion of political scientists actually think of themselves as scientists only in a figurative sense.

19. Doctoral programs in political science stress techniques rather than broad understanding and cultivation.

20. Political scientists do not devote enough attention to contemporary public policy matters.

21. Behavioralism mistakes mid-twentieth-century American institutions and character for universals.

22. Political scientists seem not to engage in studies in which one man can replicate the findings of another.

23. Much of the work being done in political behavior is only marginally related to political science.

24. The really significant problems of political life cannot be successfully attacked by the behavioral approach.

25. The American political scientist has in recent years become increasingly concerned with the adequacy of his methodology.

26. Every doctoral candidate in political science should have thorough training in the scope and method of the discipline.

27. Every doctoral candidate in political science should have thorough training in the history of political thought.

C. Here are some additional items on which we would like to have your opinion:

1. Which political scientists have made the most significant contributions to the discipline

    a. before World War II?

    b. since World War II?

2. Which fields of political science have been influenced by the behavioral approach
    a. the most?
    b. the least?

3. In which field(s) of political science is the *most* significant work now being done?

4. In which field(s) of political science is the *least* significant work now being done?

5. To what extent do you think that publication in each of the following journals contributes to professional prestige in political science? (Check "a great deal," "some," "not much," "not at all," or "can't say.")
    a. *Administrative Science Quarterly*
    b. *American Behavioral Scientist*
    c. *American Political Science Review*
    d. *Journal of Politics*
    e. *Midwest Journal of Politics*
    f. *Political Science Quarterly*
    g. *Public Administration Review*
    h. *Public Opinion Quarterly*
    i. *Western Political Quarterly*
    j. *World Politics*
    k. other (specify)

6. To what extent do you think each of the following factors contributes to a person's professional success in political science? (Check "a great deal," "some," "not much," "none," or "can't say.")
    a. school at which doctorate was taken
    b. volume of publication
    c. quality of publication
    d. performance as a teacher
    e. luck or chance
    f. having the right connections
    g. other (specify)

7. How would you characterize the over-all quality of the doctoral program in political science now offered at each

of these universities? (Check "excellent," "good," "fair," "poor," or "can't say.")

American	Northwestern
Catholic	Notre Dame
Calif. (Berk.)	N.Y.U.
Calif. (U.C.L.A.)	North Carolina
Chicago	Ohio State
Columbia	Pennsylvania
Cornell	Princeton
Duke	Stanford
Fordham	Syracuse
Georgetown	Texas
Harvard	Washington (Seattle)
Illinois	Wisconsin
Indiana	Yale
Iowa	other
Johns Hopkins	other
Michigan	other
Minnesota	

D. If there are any areas that you feel we have covered inadequately or overlooked, we would appreciate your comments about them in the space which follows.

-B-2-
Final Questionnaire

QUESTIONNAIRE ON THE STATE OF AMERICAN POLITICAL SCIENCE[1]

A. Background Data
   1. Year of birth:
   2. Year of degree(s) and name of school(s) awarding degree:

Degree	Year of degree	School
B.A., B.S., etc.		
M.A., M.S., etc.		
Ph.D.		
other		

[1] The questionnaire has been edited slightly to conform with the style of the text.

3. If you had to identify yourself with a *single* field in political science, which one would it be?

B. The following observations have been made in the past few years in the literature dealing with the state of the discipline. On the whole, how do you feel about each of them? (Check "agree strongly," "agree," "disagree," "disagree strongly," or "can't say.")

1. Much that passes for scholarship in political science is superficial or trivial.

2. Political scientists in the United States are unhappy about the current state of their discipline.

3. Political science cannot be said to have any generally agreed upon body of methods and techniques.

4. Much research in political science is undertaken simply because the projects lend themselves to research by a fashionable tool or because financial support can be readily secured.

5. By and large, the preparation of a doctoral dissertation in political science is not an intellectually satisfying experience.

6. The *American Political Science Review* currently devotes an unduly large amount of space to materials reflecting a behavioral approach.

7. Communication among political scientists tends to be seriously hindered by the inadequacy of their basic concepts.

8. Political scientists tend to be unsophisticated about the nature of scientific investigation.

9. Efforts to formulate, refine, and clarify concepts and to obtain agreement on labels to be attached to concepts often result in little more than hairsplitting and jargon.

10. The articles currently being published in the *APSR* are of a generally better quality than those published before World War II.

11. The involvement of political scientists in nonscholarly activities has tended to impede the development of the discipline.

12. A substantial part of the intellectual conflict in American political science is rooted in issues that are methodological in character.

13. Doctoral programs in political science stress research training at the cost of preparing effective undergraduate teachers.

14. The mood of contemporay American political science is one of stock-taking and self-criticism.

15. Given the present state of political science, efforts to develop a general theory of politics are premature.

16. American political science has developed an Establishment which largely determines the character and standards of the discipline.

17. A high proportion of political scientists actually think of themselves as scientists only in a broad and figurative sense.

18. Doctoral programs in political science stress techniques rather than broad understanding and cultivation.

19. By and large, political scientists do not devote enough attention to contemporary public policy matters.

20. Political science has generally competed rather successfully with the other social sciences in areas of common interest and study.

21. Political scientists seem not to engage in studies in which it is possible for one investigator to replicate the findings of another.

22. Much of the work being done in political behavior is only marginally related to political science.

23. The really significant problems of political life cannot be successfully attacked by the behavioral approach.

24. The American political scientist has in recent years become increasingly concerned with the adequacy of his methodology.

25. Every doctoral candidate in political science should have systematic training in the history of political thought.

26. There has developed an inner group in the American Political Science Association which, in large part, controls the key panel assignments at the annual Association meetings.

C. Here are some additional items on which we would like to have your opinion:

1. In your judgment, which political scientists have made the *most* significant contributions to the discipline
    a. from 1900–1945?
    b. from 1945 to present?

2. In your opinion, which fields of political science have been influenced by the behavioral approach
    a. the *most?*
    b. the *least?*

3. In which field(s) of political science do you think the *most* significant work is now being done?

4. In which field(s) of political science do you think the *least* significant work is now being done?

5. To what extent do you think that publication in each of the following journals contributes to professional prestige in political science? (Check "a great deal," "some," "very little," "not at all," or "can't say.")
    a. *Administrative Science Quarterly*
    b. *American Behavioral Scientist*
    c. *American Political Science Review*
    d. *Journal of Politics*
    e. *Midwest Journal of Politics*
    f. *Political Science Quarterly*
    g. *Public Administration Review*
    h. *Public Opinion Quarterly*
    i. *Western Political Quarterly*
    j. *World Politics*
    k. law reviews and journals
    l. other (specify)

6. To what extent do you think each of the following factors contributes to a political scientist's ability to get offers from other schools? (Check "a great deal," "some," "very little," "none," or "can't say.")
    a. school at which doctorate was taken
    b. volume of publication
    c. quality of publication
    d. teaching ability
    e. luck or chance

     f . having the right connections

     g. school of first full-time appointment

     h. textbook authorship

     i. self-promotion ("brass")

     j. ability to get research support

     k. other

7. How would you characterize the over-all quality of the doctoral program in political science now offered at each of these universities? (Check "excellent," "good," "fair," "poor," or "can't say.")

American	Northwestern
Catholic	Notre Dame
Calif. (Berk.)	N.Y.U.
Calif. (U.C.L.A.)	North Carolina
Chicago	Ohio State
Columbia	Pennsylvania
Cornell	Princeton
Duke	Stanford
Fordham	Syracuse
Georgetown	Texas
Harvard	Washington (Seattle)
Illinois	Wisconsin
Indiana	Yale
Iowa	Vanderbilt
Johns Hopkins	Michigan State
Michigan	George Washington
Minnesota	other

D. 1. If you were able to start over and pick your profession again, would you still choose a career in political science? (Check "definitely yes," "probably," "can't say," "probably not," or "definitely not.")

     2. In your opinion, what significant issues now confront the profession?

E. If there are any areas that you feel have been inadequately covered or overlooked on this questionnaire, we would appreciate your comments.

-C-
A Modest Proposal

This appendix is devoted to a need which American political scientists have largely ignored—that of studying their profession and themselves.[1] We shall touch on three closely related problems: the areas of political science which could most profitably be investigated, the necessity of securing comparable data for other disciplines, and the manner in which such an inquiry might be organized and supported.

INQUIRY INTO POLITICAL SCIENCE ITSELF

For purposes of discussion, we can identify several areas where future investigation would be particularly fruitful. They are (1) the

[1] For a stimulating if largely intuitive commentary on some of the areas that need investigation, see Harold D. Lasswell, *The Future of Political Science* (New York: Atherton Press, 1963).

recruitment of graduate students, (2) doctoral programs, and (3) the practitioner and the profession. The subtopics under each of these headings suggest only some of the directions which inquiry might take. They do not constitute a detailed blueprint or prospectus.

The Recruitment of Graduate Students

The character of a discipline, one can reasonably assume, is shaped by the type of person it attracts. The character of political science today is undoubtedly related to the recruitment that took place during the 1930's, 1940's, and 1950's. What it will be two decades from now is a function of the sort of student—indeed a sobering thought—political science is currently enlisting. Yet very little is known about the forces that attract students to political science or of the qualities of mind and personality which incline them to build a career in the profession.

Data reported during the past few years suggest that intelligence and aptitude may be selective factors in picking an academic discipline.[2] But none of these studies controlled enough of the critical parameters so that we can be reasonably certain of this. What would adequately structured inquiry reveal? Intelligence and aptitude aside, is there any special configuration of psychological traits that distinguish graduate students in political science from those, say, in economics, history, or sociology?[3] What part do the students' undergraduate experiences play in this determination? When is this choice most often made? Are there differences here between students who take their baccalaureates at a university and those who earn their degrees at undergraduate institutions? A long-standing lament in the profession has been that political science loses the best of its undergraduate majors to the law schools.

[2] Sibley, *op. cit.*, pp. 78–82.
[3] Pioneering work in this area is reported by George G. Stern, Morris I. Stein, and Benjamin S. Bloom in *Methods in Personality Assessment* (Glencoe, Ill.: Free Press, 1956).

Political scientists report that this pattern has recently begun to change. If so, how much and under what circumstances?

Once the student has decided on political science, what factors influence the selection of a graduate school? To what extent and for what type of student does the availability of scholarship and fellowship assistance affect this choice? How many graduate students have any conception of the consequences which may follow from their decision? Are there advisers, especially at the smaller, "out of the way" colleges, sufficiently familiar with the various departments to give them sound guidance?

These questions bring us to the expectations and aspirations with which the prospective Ph.D. begins his work and to the subject of doctoral programs in political science.

Doctoral Training

Graduate education (here used synonymously with doctoral training) has two quite different objectives. The first, and the one of which teachers tend to be more consciously aware, is that of transmitting to the student the requisite subject-matter knowledge and expertise. The other, less formally organized, is that of inculcating the values and beliefs which enable the student to identify himself with his chosen profession and to play with conviction, as well as with competence, the various roles inherent in its practice. Each of these objectives may be assessed from several vantage points —that of the faculty, of the deans and other educational administrators, and of the students themselves. The last mentioned has received least attention. It deserves much more.

This is not to argue that doctoral programs should be tailored to the opinions of those who at best are talented amateurs. We do suggest, though, that casual faculty impressions and observations are not an infallible guide to what students really think and that a better knowledge of their views might be very helpful in evaluating these programs and in considering policy alternatives.

What, for example, is the relationship between the students' expectations of graduate study and the reality encountered in the classroom? Are students satisfied with the level and relevance of their courses and seminars at the several stages of training? Do many drop out or perform less adequately than they might because they have not been able to develop a true sense of identification with the profession? How do they evaluate the fairness and selectivity of the ponderous apparatus of oral, written, preliminary, screening, comprehensive, and final examinations? Do the language requirements make any more sense to them than to their teachers? How does the dissertation look from a worm's-eye view? To be sure, we might ultimately dismiss their ideas as immature and superficial even when we had all this information at hand; still, as a distinguished political scientist once observed, those who partake of the meal are not without some basis for judging how well it was cooked.

The type of questions listed above should be asked at two points and of two groups: first, of students actually in the process of attaining their degrees; second, of those who took doctorates within the past three or four years and who have since had a chance to reflect on their experience. Both Berelson and Sibley afford suggestive examples of how an outside investigator can be used to advantage in this area.

The Practitioner and the Profession

We would not have undertaken this investigation unless we believed that the discipline should subject itself to systematic self-analysis. It is only natural, then, that we reaffirm the importance of keeping up-to-date the profession's knowledge of where its members stand on the professional and intellectual issues of the day.

Subsequent studies will undoubtedly be able to improve on our research design. Of some inadequacies we are all too aware. Were the inquiry to be repeated, the first change made (assuming the availability of funds and time) would be to provide for large-scale systematic interviewing. Questionnaires are valuable instruments, but there are nuances of meaning which can be much more satisfactorily resolved in face-to-face communication. Furthermore, respondents are often understandably reluctant to commit to paper opinions which they are willing to express orally.

This investigation, moreover, dealt only with certain aspects of the discipline. We made no attempt, for example, to examine the social origins of American political scientists, their political and economic ideas, or any of the other topics commonly subsumed under the rubric "sociology of knowledge."[4] The technical difficulties of working in this area are admittedly formidable. Nevertheless, the relationships between who we are and what we believe, on the one hand, and what we do and how we do it, on the other, are too important to be indefinitely ignored.

There is certainly an abundance of readily manageable subjects to which attention could profitably be devoted, given the research tools already available. Little has been done in studying career patterns among political scientists—for example, how, why, and where they move. What changes are being effected in this pattern by the current demand for Ph.D.'s? Obviously, this can be determined only by the compilation and analysis of a sizable number of representative cases.

To turn from the practitioner to the profession, an adequate intellectual history of the discipline remains to be written. The problems and issues to which this volume has been devoted could be much better comprehended if we possessed a fuller knowledge of the forces and movements in American political science from which they stem. A companion and hardly less valuable undertaking would be a history of the American Political Science Association.

Investigators who prefer to work in the present rather than the past might ask: What is our standing as a profession in the eyes of other social scientists? What strengths and weaknesses do they impute to political science? If opinions vary from discipline to discipline, wherein and why? What sort of "image," to employ a fashionable term, do public officials or the public have of political scientists? Although it is essential to know what political scientists

[4] Henry A. Turner, Charles B. Spaulding, and Charles McClintock, "Political Orientations of Academically Affiliated Sociologists," *Sociology and Social Research*, XLVII (1963), 273–289.

think of themselves, it may be equally profitable to sound the views of others.

A majority of political scientists, we have seen, believe that there is an inner group which strongly influences, in one respect or another, their professional lives. Is there *really* a powerful Establishment in American political science? How is it structured? What functions does it serve? How effective is its control? There is a nice irony in the fact that a discipline which talks so much about "power," "influence," and "elites" has been so slow to apply these concepts to a study of its own organizational behavior. As someone has aptly observed, inquiry as well as charity should begin at home.

Finally, lest this become an altogether tedious catalogue, political scientists with a taste for applied research might concern themselves with the long-range consequences of progressively expanding Ph.D. production. They have before them the example of the doctors of medicine who profess to see an analogous problem simply as one of ensuring high-quality medical training. Or, descending slightly from this high moral plane, political scientists might approach the matter as a practical matter of ensuring both a quality product *and* a judicious balance between supply and demand. There is, after all, deplorably little demand for political scientists outside the academic community, and there is not much reason to expect a drastic change in the situation. If the present trend persists, what will be the Ph.D. output by 1975—and what will then be the market for this output? As a learned profession, political science may largely do as it wishes in turning out doctorates, but the decision should be a calculated and rational one, rather than a passive and unthinking submission to the tide of events.[5]

THE NEED FOR INTERDISCIPLINARY DATA

There is hardly any need to dwell at length on the desirability of data which would make it possible to compare developments in

---

[5] On this point, a leading anthropologist writes: "This responsibility [that of ensuring appropriate positions for new Ph.D.'s in anthropology]

political science with those in history, anthropology, psychology, sociology, and economics. In past chapters, we have repeatedly mentioned the difficulty of interpreting findings in the absence of comparable evidence from other disciplines. In the rare instances where such data are at hand, analysis can take on new dimensions. Two examples should suffice. We found that many political scientists do not think very highly of the adequacy of their profession. Whether this is cause for concern depends in good part on whether economists, sociologists, or psychologists feel the same way about *their* disciplines—and this we do not know. On the other hand, the availability of roughly comparable findings on career satisfaction among sociologists warranted inferences which would not have been defensible had there been evidence for only a single discipline.

Procuring comparable data for other disciplines is hardly a chore which political scientists should themselves undertake. Nor, in fact, should this responsibility be assumed by any single profession. Practical considerations of funds and man power aside, a discipline is so complex and intricate that only those intimately familiar with it are likely to succeed in the venture. Interdisciplinary cooperation, with individual investigation pursuing commonly selected objectives, would seem to be the most viable procedure. To say this is one thing; to carry it out quite another. We come, thus, to the final problem.

THE TASK OF IMPLEMENTATION

Who is to bell the cat? How? Fair questions, indeed. The answers, we would say, depend less on the nature of the cat than on the type of bell one has in mind. There are, obviously, two tasks involved: (1) interdisciplinary cooperation to ensure comparability

---

serves as an automatic restraint on training more anthropologists than can be employed. Of course, this restraint is not an organized one. It is a covert and indirect process. . . . The net effect is that a rough balance exists between the training and the placement of professionals." Cora DuBois, "Anthropology: Its Present Interests," in Bernard Berelson, ed., *The Behavioral Sciences Today* (New York: Harper & Row, 1963), p. 28.

of data and (2) organizing and structuring inquiry within political science itself.

Interdisciplinary Cooperation

Only a single course seems feasible here—the cooperating social sciences would have to agree both on general objectives and on the manner in which each would pursue these objectives. Arrangements could be negotiated by the officials of the various associations or by a special interdisciplinary committee created for the purpose. We do not know whether such agreement could be obtained, but this would seem to be the level at which it would necessarily have to be explored.

Inquiry within American Political Science

Ideally, we might think in terms of a single massive task-force type of inquiry sponsored by the Association itself. But this does not mean that sponsorship and control should go hand in hand. There are a number of rather touchy areas—for example, that of the Establishment—where the findings of an Association-directed study, however fair-minded and impartial, might be received with some skepticism by some of the members. Divorcing financial support from actual control is not easy, but it is by no means impossible.

Another and perhaps more realistic alternative is that different aspects of the study be undertaken by investigators functioning independently of one another. The manifest advantages of this tactic are partially offset by the danger that the several inquiries may lack a common structure, that the data will not be comparable, and that some topics will be duplicated while others are passed over. Again, the problem is difficult but not insoluble.

We finally come to what is perhaps the nub of the matter, underwriting the costs of the investigation, however structured. The ultimate responsibility for securing this support rests, we believe, with the Association itself. No approach to a foundation by a single scholar or group of scholars would carry the weight of an official Association proposal. We are aware that the Association has not been able to secure funds in the past. But other professional groups —most recently the sociologists—have been able to secure grants for this purpose.

Perhaps the Association has not effectively conveyed to the appropriate foundations a precise understanding of what it wishes to accomplish and how it plans to go about the task. If American political scientists are persuaded that such a study is desirable, the formulation of a proposal to this end would seem to be the next order of business.

Index